# DEFAULT TO RESPONSIBILITY

WOMEN'S PLIGHT DURING COVID-19 AND THE SOLUTION TO REACHING EQUALITY

## WRITTEN BY:
*Brielle Valle*

---

*Foreword: By Gloria Feldt*

*For the women who let me in; for the women who paved a path.*

*For my advocates and mentors.*

*For the men who are willing to listen and learn; for the women who persevere.*

*For the young who go beyond.*

--

*And for my steadfast other half, may we continue to march forth, together.*

# CONTENTS

**06** | FOREWORD BY: GLORIA FELDT

**10** | NOTE FROM THE AUTHOR

**11** | INTRODUCTION

**15** | **I: AMERICA'S <PROMISING> DREAM**

**16** | A Timeline: Changes in the Workplace and Across Civilization Meet Few Changes in the Home

**20** | The Other Side of the Sandstorm

**22** | The World Resisted Change: Women Decided to Change Themselves

**24** | **II: WORKING FROM HOME: AN ANOMALY CHANGED NECESSITY**

**26** | The False Perception of Women Having it All

**30** | Everyone Is Online

**32** | **III: DEFAULT TO RESPONSIBILITY**

**36** | Women May Be From Venus, and Men From Mars, but Both Belong in the Solar System

**40** | Why Corporations Must Recognize Default to Responsibility

**42** | Organizational Creativity: How Corporations Will Help Society Reach Gender Equality

**46  IV: CULTURE AND UPBRINGING**

**46**  Confidence: From Childhood to the Workforce

**49**  La Familia

**50**  Society's Judgement

**53**  Media

**55  V: AN INDEPENDENT LIFE**

**59  VI: PERSISTENT INEQUITIES**

**59**  Invisible Work and Responsibility Refusal

**62**  Asking for Help

**64**  Earning

**67**  Black Lives Matter

**69**  A Sea of Emotions

**73  VII: A RELIANT LIFE**

**78  VIII: WHERE WE GO FROM HERE**

**78**  Reaching Recovery

**79**  Solutions to Implement

**85**  The Spreadsheet Solve: A Model for Equitable Parenting

**86**  Be Part of the (R)evolution

**89  DEMOGRAPHICS AND LIMITATIONS**

# FOREWORD

BY GLORIA FELDT

As closures ensued at the start of the 2020 global pandemic, I remember speaking with colleagues and professional contacts alike, Brielle Valle included, about my deep concern for what this pandemic meant for women. The warning signs were flashing early on as children had to school at home and the economy took a dive.

One year has gone by, and as we wait for broad availability of vaccines, we continue to see the daily mortality toll from COVID-19, along with spiking mental health concerns across the nation. I'm watching women leave their careers through job losses and the pressures of caregiving responsibility that falls disproportionately on their shoulders. Current job reports find four times as many women as men leaving the workforce, with the preponderance of those losses being to women of color who were already in fragile economic conditions.

Helaine Olen, opinion columnist, recently wrote in the Washington Post, "Decades from now, women will still be worse off — all because of what happened to them in 2020." For a woman like me, this is extremely discouraging. I have built my career – at least a lifetime's worth – on helping women see their own strength, power, and abilities. Making sure they know they can use it to change their life and the lives of others for the better. That's because as a young woman, society discouraged me and other women like me from aspiring to careers let alone leadership. As I became aware of the injustice of discrimination preventing half the population from achieving its potential, crafting tools for women to thrive in the world as it is while changing it to the world we want became my life's mission. This culminated in my cofounding Take The Lead, a nonprofit organization with the bold intention to reach gender parity in leadership by 2025. And we were moving forward apace. Then boom: the pandemic shook our world.

In *Default to Responsibility*, Valle chips away at just how we got here. How, she asks, with all of the ground covered and obstacles conquered in fighting for equality can it be unraveling at the seams? Valle frames the conversation by drawing upon historical influences, biological differences, and psychological dispositions. She ties the current crisis to corporations' inability to address the crisis itself.

Valle surmises that achieving and sustaining equality has everything to do with crisis preparation and crisis recovery, and it is the organizations for which women and men work that are responsible for creating an equitable future. Not only through better support of women, but through better support of men, enabling families to share the workload. If we want to reach equality, it is not up to women alone to figure out how to level the playing field. It is up to women and men together to rewrite the rules of responsibility relating to domestic work, childcare, and overarching family obligations. According to Valle, this can only happen through broad stroke change – through a commitment from organizations.

Prior to the pandemic, women were making significant progress in the workplace. The persistence and strength of a woman was paying off. But just as that woman took the next step, a crisis pushed her, sending her spiraling down and she's been trying to grab hold of any sequential rung. We are at the precipice of reverting to an undesirable world – a world from which I came. Akin to a time when I could not get a car loan without the approval and signature of my then husband. A time when women governing their own bodies and the decisions made about them was a monumental feat. A time when seeing a woman in the boardroom was rare... Pushing women out of the workplace removes not only their physical presence but also their voice.

Without a shared ideal of equality, women are set up to fail, being pushed out of the workforce and defaulting to responsibility for what should be shared.

With each published work about COVID-19 and the surrounding implications, few have offered solutions – though some have – and others place the topic on display as if this moment in time is an anomaly. I assure you it is not. We have been here before; inequity of such proportion has been no stranger. But with what we know, the problems having been laid bare, let us not fall prey to focusing solely on them but rather leverage the moment to create change, perhaps to test out a variety of solutions. *Default to Responsibility* goes to the source of the unrest and makes a case for solutions that can be readily implemented both within the workplace and within the home.

Sustained change will not happen in isolation and it surely will not happen without effort. *Default to Responsibility* outlines just some of those efforts and unveils the truth about how women have taken on the weight of the world not by choice, but by default. Through educating the decision makers of corporations to take action to right the wrong, women will excel at work, families will remain intact, and the economy will stabilize. Together, and with the help of Valle's research, decades from now women will not be worse off because of what happened in 2020 but rather will have taken the lead to create a healthier and more prosperous world for all.

---

**Gloria Feldt**
Co-Founder and President of *Take The Lead* (www.taketheleadwomen.com)

Author of:
- No Excuses: 9 Ways Women Can Change How We Think About Power
- Intentioning: Sex, Power, Pandemics and How Women Will Take The Lead
  [*Release date forthcoming*]

# NOTE FROM THE AUTHOR

In my journey of naming an unnamed and timeless but optimistically time-bound issue, I aimed to seek understanding. I wanted to draw upon historical context, personal recounts, and set forth conclusions based on both proven points and my analysis of unqueried mindsets.

A global pandemic forced entrenched inequities to bubble to the surface. And here we stand, facing a crisis that has been debilitating to women. But COVID-19 is just one of many crises to come and thus we must focus on seeking solutions.

Early in this publication, I will share a framework for understanding *default to responsibility*, prior to defining its meaning. I assert why what I discovered is a powerful learning and how, if we ever plan to get out of this mess, we must pivot and proceed forward.

Understanding *default to responsibility* requires humility and empathy – two traits that would serve us well to employ more often. Stay committed to reading these pages; this publication may just change the way you think about the world, and your role within it.

# INTRODUCTION

The World Health Organization declared the coronavirus ("COVID-19") outbreak a global pandemic on March 11, 2020. The virus posed new challenges to families, individuals, organizations, and the economy, all of which are continuing to evolve with newfound intricacies and ambiguous turns ahead.

As the world acclimated to an unforeseen reality – an evolving process still in flux – themes became abundantly clear. Jobs were lost. Unemployment swelled by more than 14 million in three months' time. Adults struggled with mental health at alarming rates. Friends, family, and countrymen lost their lives to the virus.

All the while, the nation was under duress. Political myopia and conspicuous hues of hate unraveled and then crumbled in front of us.

It was in the early weeks of risk, as a Manhattan-based individual, I was keenly aware of fear, stress, exhaustion, and uncertainty... And it was only the beginning.

It is with time we glean perspective. The perspective I aimed to hone, which consequently brought forth this publication, was to understand and share the reality of what women face during the pandemic. I envisioned restless days and nights, mothers left with a disproportionate burden to address all invisible work, and corporations offering little empathy to men and women with children. I am here to share that my imagined circumstances were not creative. They were wistfully not far from reality.

It is my desideratum to educate men, women, and organizations about the essentiality of gender equity. It is not a piece of the puzzle; it is a cyclical flow. Each curved edge is required to bring about change and push us forward with momentum to achieve progress. While this study includes participants from countries outside of the United States of America, the majority of women interviewed presently reside in the United States and are subject to gender inequality in this still immature facet of our nation. I am adamant that we must peek under the antiquated hood of gender roles, evaluating the engine that has been constantly running, and forced to churn amidst chill and heat, its composition no longer sustainable for the terrain.

Researchers, authors, activists, and many others, have chipped away at freeing the restrained engine from inequity. With age, bolts loosen and wires fray. The engine becomes weary. If the engine is representative of a woman bearing the weight of a successful career, childcare, and home making, it seems evident we need more support not only for the engine, but in cultivating new ways of cracking open the stifling hood. The hood is representative of a culture with unchanged antediluvian constructs. Pervicacious as this may show me to be, I am convinced there is a different – and better – way to live. A reality where the engine is optimized to run, removing the disproportionate burden from women who are so frequently the ones to keep the car operating.

This story is filled with others' stories: Women's experiences, thoughts, and observations about what it means to be female during the COVID-19 global pandemic. It is these anecdotes that allow for critical evaluation of the present, and act as a catalyst for change. These accounts also permit clarity, giving us a glimpse of the work that needs to be done to craft a more favorable future, disseminating responsibility across individuals instead of the singular, and rethinking our own implicit *default to responsibility* within family life.

# STUDY BRIEF

The purpose of this study was to understand how the COVID-19 pandemic is affecting women's equality. I used ethnographic research, a qualitative methodology, to comprehend the changes in how women spent their time. I obtained information about the socio-cultural phenomena of the 2020 global pandemic through observation and interviews. I investigated what adjustments were taking place, not only in the home but in the workplace. I sought to understand both the mental health implications of the global pandemic and what feelings women had, with children and without, about being a female during this time. I gained insight into the additional responsibilities that were assumed, learned how earning potential was being affected, and captured the reality of experienced mental and physical exhaustion.

The 66 women interviewed for this study[1] were asked a series of 27 questions about their personal account from the onset of the pandemic to present day. Excerpts from interviewees are included within this publication, using categorical pseudonyms to maintain anonymity. As a result of archaic constructs about gender roles and entrenched inequity, I predicted the effects of COVID-19 were ravaging women due to the disproportionate amount of labor being inflicted upon them. Through data capture and review, I achieved an outcome of proposed solutions and recommendations about how to lead families and organizations forward to achieve gender parity.

---

[1] Demographic data, limitations, and confidentiality details are provided on page 89.

# I: AMERICA'S <PROMISING> DREAM

"The American Dream," as we broadly know it, is about the prospect of success. Yet, 100 years ago the phrase meant something different from what the collective currently holds it to mean. The original American Dream was not a dream of individual wealth; instead, it was a dream of equality, justice, and democracy for the nation.

## IF ONLY WE HAD THE PROSPICIENCE TO SUBSCRIBE TO THIS VISION FOR THE PAST CENTURY...

Sarah Churchwell found that the saying "American Dream" was repurposed by each generation until the Cold War. At that time, it became the defense for a consumer capitalist variation of democracy. After that, the meaning was not seemingly multivocal. That is until about two years ago, in 2019, when a sizable *New York Times* survey was conducted to capture the present meaning of the American Dream. According to survey results, rather than representing the prized jewel of monetary success, the meaning has shifted: American's new dream is a freedom of choice in how to live and how to have a good family life. Simply put, choice is the driver in one's pursuit of happiness.

## A TIMELINE:
## CHANGES IN THE WORKPLACE AND ACROSS CIVILIZATION MEET FEW CHANGES IN THE HOME

In search of economic stability, the Industrial Revolution poised American men for earning in a capacity that was efficient. While women did perform work during this period, they earned one-third to one-half of a man's average salary. Even as industry grew, women earned a minuscule amount compared to men. It was the inception of pay inequity, at scale, for Americans. The uprisal of the Industrial Revolution simultaneously led to a reality in which women became more subjugated to men. Men earning wages for the family quickly became the standard and represented the ideal America during the Industrial Revolution; this confined women to work solely within the home and ensured little potential for a female's financial freedom.

Part of the American Dream placed a responsibility of earning and earning potential on men. While men were groomed and enabled to become providers, there were notable advancements for women, mainly starting in the 1920s. Women were granted the right to vote, began to retire corsets and long skirts, and commenced exploration of sexual freedom, thanks to the tenacity of Margaret Sanger. Women started to take jobs as clerks, teachers, and nurses. The uptick in job placement related directly to women's access to education which continued to prosper.

For context, in the beginning of 2020 women earned more than 57% of all undergraduate degrees and 61% of all master's degrees. They earned 51% of all law degrees and 50.5% of all medical degrees. They accounted for 50.4% of the U.S. labor force and 52.5% of the college-educated workforce. And these percentages were continuing to rise year-over-year for females. That is until the COVID-19 pandemic.

Although women were starting to work in non-labor positions as a result of increased education beginning in the 20th century, they were placed into supportive, non-decision-making roles. Definitionally, females became subordinated to their male counterparts.

In the 10-year period between 1929 and 1939, the epoch of the Great Depression, women searched for employment in order to assist their husbands, who had either lost their jobs or were also looking for work. However, even when the nation was in disarray and it was a challenge to put food on the table, for all, women were ostracized for working. Women were taking jobs from men and were expected to "give them back" should a man need a job to support his family. In one of the direst times in the post-Industrial America, families were reliant on each member pitching in to earn a living, but the country was still intent on resorting to the ingrained gender roles of its past.

The tone was not dissimilar in the following World War II years. Women assumed men's positions to not only prevent economic collapse, but to provide for themselves and their families. When husbands returned, if in fact they did, women were told to step aside. Women were merely a temporary placeholder for men's careers.

In a not-so-distant history, the American culture did not broadly see women as professional equals. In fact, women were only viewed as useful in the working world, historically speaking, when that decision was made by men and on a predefined timetable. In addition to being a culture built on pay inequity, the opportunity to work and the sheer ability to provide for oneself or family was relatively inaccessible for women. Temporary societal and economic pressures, like those of World War II, demanded that women learn new skills for the purpose of earning, adding to their in-home knowledge. Men, on the other hand, were not expected to learn the skills of being a homemaker or care provider, at least not on a mass scale within our country's history. While women were seen as a professional afterthought, they were also exposed to varying professions and their career horizons were broadened (even if the reasoning was dysfunctional). Women demonstrated capability in not only managing a home, but also in holding a job. Perhaps the recognition of such capability is where the trouble ballooned.

The 1950s was the era of the white picket fence, an iconic symbol of American culture: The picturesque white, middle class, suburban life, with a heterosexual marriage and at least two children. The deviation of an American Dream that sought for equality and justice 50 years prior seemed but a faint memory at this juncture. The children of this time, baby boomers, were the result of the end of World War II. It is believed that traditionalists aimed to protect their children (boomers) from the discomfort of their own life experiences, e.g., The Great Depression and world war. War leads to destruction, death, and heartache, and traditionalists – those who were born before the year 1945 – had an opportunity to repair the world in which they lived. This repair took shape through a glamourized lens of the perfect family: The white picket fence and the return to some form of known normalcy.

The 1960s brought with it crusaders. Women marched for equal pay. They spoke against domestic violence, which paved a path to the establishment of shelters and crisis hotlines for battered women (these came to be in the 1970s, yet our nation still faces domestic violence rates at the clip of one in four in 2021). Women also made major strides against sexual harassment in the workplace, generating environments where women could work without guaranteed fear of misconduct. The topic of equitable division for housework and child rearing was prevalent, too. Change was necessary, but not imminent.

It was not until 1972 that women were allowed to keep their maiden names when married. At that time, the law recognized one person in married couples, and that person was the husband. This yielded ownership to him of property and finances.

A woman's identity was swiftly wiped away, as she assumed the man's first and last name along with a new salutation: "Mrs. John Doe." Identity is defined as "the fact of being who or what a person or thing is." It is the amalgamation of experiences, education, feelings, and appearance. A woman could be met with scrutiny for wanting to uphold her personal identity.

*The audacity.*

---

What I ask of men is this: Consider taking your wife's last name. If this feels appalling, we have a lot of ground to cover. What I ask of women is this: Do not give in to a wish that is not your own. Be remembered and be memorable. It is time to adjourn the assumed patriarch.

---

The list of milestones achieved each decade by women is far more exhaustive than what I am including hereto, but there maintains a recurring theme: A woman's pursuit of knowledge, fair treatment, and autonomy. From the Women's Business Ownership Act of 1988 – which put an end to state laws requiring women to have male relatives sign business loans – to the Breastfeeding Amendment – which ensured that funds would not be used to prohibit women from breastfeeding their children in Federal buildings or on Federal property in the 1990s – the accomplishments continue on.

## THE OTHER SIDE OF THE SANDSTORM

We live in an arguably sophisticated society. From earning potential, to transportation forms, to the ability and optionality for procreation, the United States continues its evolution, albeit in a "two steps forward" and "one step back" manner.

Dissonance exists between the ideal of equality, which was the initial construct of the American Dream, and the cultural reality of male dominance. Instead of a society of equality, a society was created with widespread inequitable pay for women, limitations on career alternatives, forced reliance, assured fear, and predetermined frames about women's worth, body, and purpose.

What is curious is the aforementioned statistics about education and the percentage attribution between men and women (see page 17). This points to the present picture, where women are excelling in professional and academic environments. Women hold more professional degrees than men, are breaking into previously untapped industries, and are rising the ranks. Yet women still do not have pay parity, make up only 7.4% of Fortune 500 CEOs, and occupy only 10% of top management positions in S&P 1500 companies. Considering the structural dynamics that keep women out of the workforce and in the home, as well as away from high earning potential, women are undoubtedly impressive in the ability to overcome obstacles. Females have persevered amidst judgment, enmity, and antagonistic social pressures.

Pair this understanding with the fact that women still do the brunt of the work in the home (more to come on this later). It is astonishing really: Life had a box—a box that worked for men—and women found a way to fit within it. Women were afterthoughts. *A very important afterthought, might I add.* Over the years, women found cracks in the lines that kept the structure intact. And since, women have simply been fighting for equity. The feminist of today is not aiming to see men suffer; they are seeking parity.

Our society has commenced recognition of women's achievements – even those women who no longer have an earthly presence. Women are earning promotions, higher (but still not equal) pay, and are recognized for their intelligence. Society is moving forward in essence, but defaults to its historical structures that sustain inequity.

## THE WORLD RESISTED CHANGE: WOMEN DECIDED TO CHANGE THEMSELVES

We have observed women who "wanted it all" and now "have it." But that is, quite frankly, teetering on a falsehood. Within the confines of the American norm, and without a division of labor and a recognition of finite hours in a day, women will continue to exert copious amounts of energy and will continue to do a disproportionate amount of work in the home and with children. Women are qualified to take on more responsibilities, learn more, and earn more, but this comes at a cost. Without an honest depiction of what reality looks like for women today, we will continue to struggle with how to divide time. What my research unambiguously suggests is that women who want it all will do more and sleep less – an unsustainable approach. Without our male counterparts recognizing these comprehensive issues and permeating corporate America for a paradigm shift, we will never reach equality. If we do not instill change, it is more likely than not that 10 years from now another fiery woman will do a research project and indite about the unchanged circumstances. A bleak outlook.

In a not-so-distant past, women and men had respective unexamined roles and clearly defined paths of responsibility. Life was outwardly simple in a time where females were silenced so frequently, they grew tired of fighting to be heard, and some resorted to saving their voices. Time progressed, those responsibilities so clearly shifted, and women began to use their voices with fervor. Paths got rerouted, opportunity was seized, and women embraced liberation. But that is not fully true. The expectations of women did not shift along with the changing tide of circumstance. This means that the life which was held by men was afforded to women – the life of success, earning potential, and organizational governance.

But nothing else changed.

It is high time to assess societal gender normalities along with rampant inequities, from the value of time to the use of it. We must take these principles within our organizations and homes and rewrite the rules of conduct, rethinking capacity, competence, and caretaking. If we want to not only restore the American Dream of equality, justice, and democracy, but to live a life aligning to the newly defined American Dream (having freedom of choice in how to live and how to have a good family life) we have a lot of work to do.

The *default to responsibility* burdens the female's capability to capitalize on this new American Dream. Arguably, "choice" is missing from the equation.

# II: WORKING FROM HOME: AN ANOMALY CHANGED NECESSITY

In 2009, working adults were dabbling with a less broadly known cadence: Work from home (WFH). At the time, it was considered a privilege – a notion employers allowed with strict guidelines. That is, unless the work was virtual from the get-go and/or the position required ample travel. After a year of global pandemic, this "privilege" is viewed differently. While WFH can be advantageous, overarching sentiments have changed specifically for women.

Working from home with suggested best practices is a fine way to conduct business; however, when children are brought into the picture, the idealistic WFH situation is faulty and causes significantly more stress. The pairing of technological advances has already created an expectation for employees to WFH during off-hours, whether there is a structural office or not. Technology can and has created a second shift for people everywhere. When you remove physical buildings where work is meant to occur, all boundaries are blurred. The additional after-hours work simply blends nto the day, and individuals are left with no physical barriers to even attempt to maintain a healthy perspective about the separation of work and personal life. The supplemental working hours – thanks to smart devices, personal laptops, and WiFi which can divert someone's attention in a blink of an eye – already have such prevalence in the home. Without the true segmentation of a day's work and parenting, energy is stretched thin. The findings from two separate research studies comparing men and women working from home – one conducted a decade ago and another in the present day – show a decrease of work produced only for women. One may infer why.

The reason organizations, individuals, and namely women were concerned about the stay-at-home order as an effect of COVID-19 is at least in part based on this prior research. It was predicted women's workloads would inflate, work productivity would decrease, and consequences would ensue. From decreased potential of earning a promotion to the removal of a performance-based lagniappe, women would feel the burden of working from home more than their male counterparts in cases where there are children – but this time in an unparalleled manner. The pandemic was an unfamiliar circumstance that in many cases eliminated, by necessity, the option of childcare assistance.

A recent 2020 study in the academic journal *Gender, Work & Organization* showed that in heterosexual relationships, mothers reduced their work hours four to five times more than fathers. This was true in situations where both the mother and father are employed and have children under 13. Yet, in this same time period, I only found this to be true for 30% of my participants. Instead, 70% of my participants with children maintained their level of weekly work or increased the hours worked due to high demand from COVID-19 uncertainties. In a finite 24-hour day, they did this by decreasing the number of hours slept each night. While variability in research is to be expected based on research methodology and design, both outcomes are problematic. One leaves a woman facing exhaustion and burnout. The other causes women to stay stagnant or lose footing on the ladder rung and fall behind – the same ladder they have been so diligently trying to climb since before the 20th Century.

## THE FALSE PERCEPTION OF WOMEN HAVING IT ALL

While women can technically have it all, to what end? As discussed in the prologomenal chapter, the physical and emotional effects are notable and will be discussed at even greater length. If we think back to the early to mid-2000s, a phenomenon called the Opt-Out Revolution was striking with a fury. Women were being encouraged to opt out of their jobs. At the time, the media was romanticizing the idea of leaving the workplace to help release work stress and put an emphasis back on family life.

Not too long after, the Great Recession of 2008 hit Americans with a vengeance. The women who considered being at home for a short time no longer had the luxury of easily returning to work, and they were met with a sea of competition upon an attempted return to the professional landscape. In this same vein, part of the reason the COVID-19 pandemic and the associated stay-at-home orders are concerning is based on the natural consideration that now is another good time to "take a break" from the office and focus again on family. This will undoubtedly put women at risk when it comes to earning potential and re-entering the workforce.

One participant shared with me it was hard to navigate the ever-changing threats and implications of COVID-19. This woman, Participant W, enjoys her career and has never considered staying at home to solely care for her children, yet as the months progressed, she was encouraged by both her in-laws and her parents – all of whom hold doctorate-level degrees – to take time off. While the grandparents were concerned about the young granddaughter's risk of contracting the virus from school, Participant W was aghast.

Both women who were encouraging Participant W to take a break are well-educated and career-oriented. She saw her biggest supporters deterring her from returning to work, and instead encouraged her to remain in the home. She could not reconcile the opinion or advice, as well-intended as it may have been. Is it not our duty to encourage women to remain in their careers, and instead change the way we view care and responsibility? Not one family member gave the same proposition to this participant's husband – it was not a consideration. This state of mind is intrinsically inequitable. The structural norm of American gender roles prevails and *default to responsibility* remains a woman's cross to bear.

Of the participants in my study, half shared the thought of leaving their job and staying home – even if they did not intend to act on it. "The second shift is too much to take any longer," said Participant L. Of those, 50% knew it was not financially feasible. The other 50% shared it was a daily consideration – and admitted to this with sincere dread in their voices.

They candidly stated that they did not know how much longer they could carry the responsibilities of the family along with their full-time careers.

Another participant, Participant N, is a senior executive and was amidst changing jobs to a more lucrative and senior position. As schools closed and she saw the Jenga pieces falling, she opted to decline the role, as she knew she would need to provide for her family – in the capacity of helping her children with schoolwork, making meals, and supporting her husband with the quotidian household tasks, so he could continue to put in long days, devoting his time to his career. She realized her accomplishment would need to be placed on the backburner. When we spoke over seven months into the pandemic, she was beginning to job search again. Even in that short time away, she was concerned about the job market, the known competition, and her ability to demonstrate her excellence when she had been at home for the last two quarters. But, she knew that her responsibilities as the primary care giver would preclude her from being an excellent contributor in her recently earned executive position.

Participant N is like many women I spoke with: Strong-willed, intelligent, exceptional. This perfection-seeking individual is keenly aware of pressures and expectations and aims to not fail in any regard (more on this later). Participant N was eager to re-enter the workforce, a place that provides her with achievement and respect for her expertise. It is important to note that the male CEO of the company, whom she would be working alongside, had a wife who stayed at home with their respective children. The muffled but observed fear was that he would only see parenting through his own lens – a demand that was not overwhelming or time exhaustive. It is probable he could have a comparable expectation for his new colleague.

Participant N had to choose between knowing that childcare would be her responsibility in a time of crisis – without any external help – and pursuing and excelling in her career where she was expected to not have these non-work-related duties. The decision was not made lightly.

Imagine a world where gender equity was not viewed through a supervisor's personal lens, but instead on an agreed upon spectrum that embraces shared responsibility.

Over two million women are or have considered taking a leave of absence or leaving the workforce entirely due to the COVID-19 crisis. With only a few examples, a reader can understand why. But since men significantly outnumber women in middle management, women leaving will then remove the potential for companies to promote them to senior management positions. Men will be the option. Women will have taken one giant step backwards if they leave their places of employment, losing the progress made in recent years. This is without a doubt just one reason companies must invest in gender equality. Without organizational support, women will be *forced* to leave if the workload of the second shift is not reallocated.

Whether a woman is considering returning to the home based on expectation, pressure, or burnout, there is an economic misconception about the optionality to "just stay home." It is a miraculously simplified perception of what it means to stay at home with children. The assumption is this: If you are married, the husband will provide, and thus a woman may stay at home. This dinosaur of a consideration is not near the current truth. The standards that families have in the present day, consisting of vacations, childcare, academic opportunity, extracurriculars, and so on, generally do not enable one parent to stay home. Dual income has become, more or less, a necessity. It seems like an appropriate decade to retire an ignorant and naive assumption to close the gap between today's economic realities and our *default to responsibility* history.

## EVERYONE IS ONLINE

As soon as the plight of COVID-19 began to impede upon organizational success, Participant D knew she had to look for another job, as her role at the time placed her smack dab in the travel vertical. While she knew it was a less than ideal time to seek employment, she felt she had no other choice. And she was not wrong. Following the 2001 terrorist attacks, the travel and flight-specific industry collapsed. As a point of comparison, the six biggest U.S. airlines in 2020 experienced losses nearly twice as great (inflation-adjusted) from that time. Even with governmental aid, airlines are seeing multi-million-dollar losses, as not only did entertainment travel cease, but business travel was slashed, leaving those who were fortunate enough to do so resorting to laptops and provisional office space.

Participant D shared with me that her new employer was clear about the fact they were not previously keen on WFH. Prior to COVID-19, WFH was not an option put forth by the company. But when the organization realized the landscape of working would be different in the year(s) to come, they embraced the talent pool potential and sought candidates out of state. I spoke with leaders in the technology industry, heading up teams from product to client management. They shared that the vagueness or lack of guidance from their organizations surrounding WFH is what made it challenging in the past. But now with Human Resources (HR) and People Operations teams managing and guiding best practices and policies for organizational WFH, department heads are excited about newfound recruitment potential.

In seeking to understand organizational culture with a discerning eye over the years, I have come to learn how hesitant remote working makes many managers. I was hired by a Fortune 100 company in 2018 to educate managers on just how to engage and effectively manage virtual employees. At the time, it was a circumstantial opportunity for company employees and not a necessity. Employees would complain of poor communication from management and would identify a feeling of isolation. Companies did not fully trust employees to work conscientiously from home, and at both ends of the spectrum there was conflict.

What we now know is remote working is oppositional to a lackadaisical approach. In fact, organizations gain more working hours from their staff in a WFH scenario. The way in which the current remote working phenomenon came to be is not favorable, but it is undoubtedly here to stay (even if in varied forms).

# III: DEFAULT TO RESPONSIBILITY

I am not referring to legal jargon when I say *default to responsibility*. Instead, it is a concept – a rough theory even. The sentiment is this: Females are the only human gender who can biologically carry and birth a child. It is the female who can provide for her infant as he or she learns to breathe oxygen once out of in utero. Prior to baby formula, health monitoring, and modern medicine, mothers were the sole providers of nourishment. Let us not forget how hormones also burnish a mother-child bond. Psychology professor Ruth Feldman at Bar-Ilan University in Israel, a leading expert on the effects of oxytocin, found women with higher levels of oxytocin during their first trimester are primed for creating bonding behaviors – both mental and behavioral.

It seems logical women would have an innate need to provide for the small human they created. The child is in existence to (initially) be cared for and, unlike other mammals, humans take years to develop. The human brain alone can take up to 25 years to develop fully. There are few other options than for a parent to care for their child and/or enlist help early in a child's life (and for plenty of time thereafter).

Thus, in this context, a mother's *default to responsibility* is intuitive, and easy to understand.

Let us take a parallel step to observe the *default to responsibility* for a father. While a comparable argument can be made for why men should feel similar responsibility for their children (they not only take part in the child's creation, but their hormones also change, including increased levels of oxytocin used for bonding), men do not carry or birth a child. However, an increasing amount of literature demonstrates that paternal involvement plays a vital role in not only reducing child mortality, but in improving social, psychological, and educational outcomes. Meaning, that in order for a child to receive the health and well-being benefits of paternal participation, fathers need to be present. If a person thoughtfully ratiocinates about what is best for the development of a child, they will conclude that dual parenting in equal parts is the quaesitum.

**DEFAULT TO RESPONSIBILITY IS AN IMPLIED RESPONSIBILITY BASED ON BIOLOGY AND CONDITIONING. THE HIGH REPETITION OF GENDERED TASKS FURTHER ENGRAINS ASSUMED RESPONSIBILITY SETS, ENSURING THAT WOMEN CONTINUOUSLY HAVE A DISPROPORTIONATE BURDEN OF DOMESTIC WORK AND CHILDCARE.**

Yet, fathers are seldom offered a respectable paternity leave to create a significant biological bond, further perpetuating and enforcing the *de-*

*fault to responsibility* of the mother, while simultaneously lessening the responsibility set of the father.

Although comparatively trivial, let us assume a man recently purchased a vehicle. The car is registered to his name, he has monthly payments due to the bank for a loan, and he intends to keep the car squeaky clean. The purchase is something he price-compared, considered thoughtfully, and is proud about. Month after month this man pays his bill, cleans his car, and ensures appropriate maintenance. The responsibility is his and his alone. But what if a partner purchased the car with him? What if it was a joint decision with shared resources? While it is safe to wager that each scenario looks a little different, it is reasonable to predict a division in labor for maintaining the vehicle whether that is through scheduling a tire rotation, reviewing insurance coverage, or paying for the monthly associated costs. With this logic, it is not a wild notion to assume that *default to responsibility* occurs when there is a feeling of ownership. *This is mine and therefore I must care for it.*

In the context of family planning, having children is unquestionably a shared decision. Why then is it not a *shared* responsibility?

Herein lies a key observation of this study: Why is it that women are mostly the primary care provider for their children? Why is it that women are more likely than men to also do the laundry, clean the house, prepare meals, grocery shop, wash dishes, pay bills, and plan family activities? Why is it that women are working fewer hours at their place of employment compared to their partners during this pandemic if there are children in the house? Why is it that women assume household tasks – no matter how menial – as their responsibility?

Caitlyn Collins, an assistant professor of sociology at Washington University, speculates that part of the issue may be that "when a child needs help, they go to mommy first." And given the aforementioned contributing factors that create *default to responsibility* sets between mothers and fathers, Collins' assertion is expected and unsurprising.

Participant G, a mother of three who works full time for a Fortune 100 company, shared with me that her children were placed next to her starting in the spring of 2020 when schools went solely virtual to ensure they had support throughout the day. "In general, the kids don't want to go to him [Participant G's husband] because he doesn't have patience. The adjacency to my children also ensures my inability to have undivided attention on my work... and now I am the last one to sleep, and the first one up. I get my work done, but it is often not until 2:00 a.m. when my head hits the pillow."

Seventy-five percent of participants with children shared with me their husbands retreated to a home office, makeshift or not, where there was a possibility to close doors or achieve some semblance of privacy. The recurring theme of kids going to their moms first is consistent with Collins' findings, and are also consistent with the structural factors that reinforce gender-specific responsibilities. Moms are not only the first line of defense, but my research shows fathers, in some cases, are actively not visible, not accessible, and highly resistant to help. I gathered that the point of view from the husband for some of the participants is they do not know how schooling from home "works," and do not have the patience to learn the new systems the school set into place. One participant shared her husband never even signed into their child's online schooling system. Twenty percent of women told me that they woke their school-aged children up before 5:30 a.m. each day to get in some schoolwork. This way, the child or children had a good start to the day and the mom would then be able to focus on her own work uninterrupted. They would then reconvene schooling later in the afternoon. This was only possible when the child was old enough to be somewhat independent.

Returning to the point about parent-child bonds, we need to break the cycle of this self-fulfilling prophecy. Children are born, bonds are established with the parents they are most with, and those are reinforced not only as an outcome of maternal leave and the absence of (or inadequate) paternal leave, but in the years to come, as a mother defaults to her presumed responsibility – her children. Furthermore, in the absence of equitable childcare and parental leave, women are often the sole option to address the needs of their children, and this shapes the way children think about care and where to get it. Neither the mother or father redirect the cadence, and children's neural pathways are solidified: They go to mom first. The mother is now the child's default, and the child is now the mother's disproportionate responsibility.

## WOMEN MAY BE FROM VENUS, AND MEN FROM MARS, BUT BOTH BELONG IN THE SOLAR SYSTEM

The COVID-19 pandemic has made it clearer that organizations playing an active role in gender parity is more vital than ever. In the early days of my preparation for attaining research about women's experiences during the pandemic, I was intent on the idea that crisis preparation and crisis recovery are of utmost importance for companies – not only to be transparent about what policies organizations hold when times are tough, but how compensation is affected along with flexibility and goals. McKinsey & Company found that fewer than a third of companies have adjusted their performance review criteria to account for the dramatic changes of the pandemic – a lackluster reporting.

Participant J shared with me how badly she wishes her organization would speak up and recognize how hard it is for working parents – particularly mothers. "It's the smoke in the trees but no one wants to address how to put out the fire." Participant Q later shared two formal email communications from her organization – from the male CEO – about how to utilize WFH time. The messaging made it clear that working from home is an opportunity to buckle down on projects, make more calls, and exceed targets. Participant Q said she read the first message and her heart sank. As she had one toddler on her lap, and an infant nearby napping, she knew she was about to face a challenging time ahead for the foreseeable future. Her goals did not change, comparable to the majority of women I interviewed; in fact, her work responsibilities increased during the spring 2020 lockdown. The tone from the company was not one that wanted to acknowledge the fact that some employees had children. Instead, the company not once offered a resource for working parents with children at home.

I was able to interview three department heads of HR, and there was a recurring theme. The tune was that of a perturbed c-suite when faced with the probability of needing to be more flexible than ever before. In each of these cases, there was a woman running HR, who was not in the c-suite and a male CEO. One interviewee, Participant T, shared that her efforts were more or less overlooked in the early phase of the pandemic. She was coined as "emotional" and was thought to be overreacting. "I would argue that, had it not been for my insistence, we would not have had a pandemic framework at all at my company. I also think the process was strangely gendered. I had to fight and claw to get what we got for our employees in terms of closing the office, abiding by health standards, and offering support for parents. It's almost as if the c-suite had an innate hate for struggle. It was not affecting them and thus should not affect others. The c-suite is all men, only one with a child whose wife is a stay-at-home mom." It was not until a young employee died from COVID-19 that the c-suite began to listen to Participant T's recommendations.

A lack of diversity across the executive leaders of an organization will translate into deficient policies and outcomes for a diverse workforce, especially in times of crisis.

In my research about female leaders during COVID-19, I observed that countries governed by women had a lower mortality and infection rate than those led by men. This is testament to the essentiality of reaching gender equity at the decision-making level within corporations (and in government). Women leaders were able to not only recognize the complications of full-time work and parenting, but they were able to make policies to keep more people out of harm's way. Participant G1 made a comment that struck a chord. Her familiarity with family stress, caring for sick parents, children, and even her spouse, gives her a profound sense of empathy for those who are facing sickness from COVID-19. Is it any wonder why empathy has been directly linked to effective leadership and management? What's more, she knows the weight of working full-time and managing the household, even with hired help. Her strength is one she believes most women – and unquestionably most mothers – possess: An ability to identify with others, reflect on complexities, and implement processes to reasonably support employees. "Trying to envision wearing someone else's shoes seems to be common sense, but it's the disproportionate responsibility women maintain, even amidst chaos, that enables us to do so. It isn't surprising to me women are better apt to manage crises. We're often facing one."

Another interviewee, Participant D, shared with me her prior boss's unconcealed incredulity about the pandemic as a whole. "He quite literally did not believe that COVID was a thing and would make that statement on numerous occasions. He went as far as to send me an email stating that I need to find a way to work in this new normal. If I couldn't work with my kid at home, I should consider taking additional time off." In December 2020 alone, women lost 140,000 jobs in the United States. As of January 2021, women are down one million more jobs than men since February 2020, and that is not counting "optional" departures. Yet, the most debilitating time for women in the workforce is proving advantageous for men working from home. Men received twice the pay raise in the past year, were three times more likely to be promoted, and gained additional leadership responsibility.

The very men who are being rewarded for their commitment to work, especially in the WFH environment, are benefiting from the disproportionate labor their wife is carrying, further cementing gender roles not only within families but within the workforce. Companies encouraging women to step aside and concomitantly rewarding men indirectly (or directly) for their insularity is a colossal misstep. Instead, corporations must stimulate men in the workforce to ensure equality within the home. This is a pivotal moment in time.

## WHY CORPORATIONS MUST RECOGNIZE
### *DEFAULT TO RESPONSIBILITY*

I work with an organization called WORK180. Their mission is to empower every woman to choose a workplace where they can thrive, which is why their transparent job board only features companies that meet a clear minimum benchmark. These companies must openly display their benefits and policies around parental leave, flexible working, diversity and inclusion, and more, giving women a way to ensure potential employers hold values and systems that align with their needs and expectations.

WORK180 is keenly aware of the need to empower women to make decisions about their employer, especially when it revolves around livelihood, family, and health. Women are often the individuals expected to manage family planning and all that comes along with it. If organizations turn a blind eye to the infrastructure that dictates this unfair divide of responsibility between men and women, they are contributing to the fate of women remaining in middle management at best and holding them back from the c-suite.

While the concept of gender equity has been a sociological consideration and anthropological topic in academia for over 40 years, it has mainly remained there. The grassroot approach of women, and in some cases men, educating friends and family about how to be equitable is indicative of why the change is a slow and steady drip. These efforts are warranted and unequivocally essential – yet, by definition, lack the scale that creates vast sustainable change. I have personally been the campaigner for not only myself but for colleagues, slowly chipping at the structural biases and judgments that are rampant. From pointing out sexually lewd behavior, to educating men about the astounding offensive comments rooted in stereotypical beliefs, women have been working diligently to seek change. The truth is that in our society women are required to have thick skin. These individual and grassroot efforts to effectuate change require tact, assertiveness, and comfort with conflict.

But by inserting the matter of gender equity into the organizations for which we work, broad stroke change is possible. For future generations of women to not fear retaliation from employers for identifying wrongdoing, to secure their seat in the boardroom, and to get compensated equally to male colleagues, the additional efforts of normalizing equality from within organizations will all be worth it.

Just as the integrity of a leader shapes the ethical efficacy of an organization, so too does their opinion about where women, or men, belong. It is time to leverage organizational structure and reach to educate not only employees, but to influence those who govern companies. This approach will expedite the path to equity and is the reason I conducted this research. Not only do we need to recognize current inequities – from pay to mutual respect to true corporate diversity – we need to prepare for times of crisis – those akin to a global pandemic that threatens progress and reverts behavior back to its suboptimal default.

## ORGANIZATIONAL CREATIVITY: HOW CORPORATIONS WILL HELP SOCIETY REACH GENDER EQUALITY

Organizations have the ability to be innovative – from choosing how to interact with employees to selecting company benefits to creating a culture of inclusion. In some cases, interviewees indicated their company was adaptable. What we now know is this adaptability is far ahead of the curve in crisis management. Participant P shared that her organization implemented a program for those who have children, decreasing the required number of hours worked each week for as long as employee parents did not have outside childcare. The required hours changed from eight hours a day to six hours a day. Participant P indicated that had she not been afforded this adjustment in hours, she does not know how she would have managed with her toddler alone all day. Her husband's work was essential and his schedule was unforgiving. Another participant, Participant B1, shared that her organization increased paid time off by two weeks for anyone who had children. This helped with scheduling flexibility and was a reassuring gesture of support.

Meanwhile, in a *Riveter* study, only six percent recorded their employer changing benefits to help parents during the pandemic. Further, slightly over 60% of my study's participants had a scarring experience with the company at which they were employed. Formalized company communication was in a tone of support and understanding; there was cognizance of the additional toll this was taking. What was regrettable, however, was the incongruency of action and words. Employees were told there would be flexibility and understanding when needing to adjust schedules and working different hours, but the message was at odds with the way these mothers were treated. Participant M indicated her boss would act overtly miffed when a child was on the screen during internal video meetings and felt she received retribution in the following months. Participant O experienced a newfound distaste from her boss for people who were not able to make weekly meetings or who had to reschedule client calls based on last minute changes. A salient point: There is no scheduling a child's temper tantrum. Participants who did not have support from their organizations conveyed a decrease in happiness in their marriages, high and constant stress, physical and mental exhaustion, and incredible guilt about their potentially inadequate parenting methods.

Another interviewee, Participant K, told me she and a colleague crafted a proposal for their superior, the contents of which shared a plan of temporary changes. Their team holds varying responsibilities, but the core of their roles is comparable. Participant K came up with a way for individuals without children to work in a more client-facing capacity, while those with children would assume more of the back-office work. The number of hours worked would remain the same, but the shifted responsibilities would minimize rescheduling of external meetings when family affairs commandeered plans, decrease the probability of interruptions, and would pose higher flexibility when work was completed, e.g., evening hours. The proposal was not considered nor escalated to anyone with decision making power.

Imagine if that company had a culture and foundational bedrock of gender equality and empathy, guiding supervisors when presented with value accretive ideas for the betterment of time/resource allocation and family life. Instead, a perfectly fine and creative solution never saw the light of day.

Much of what I learned is, even if a company had intentions to support parents and those with additional care responsibilities, the flexibility or lack thereof was up to the manager. It may be hard to fathom that the fate of a career relies on an individual – a manager – and not on the company as a whole and its policies. The disconnect between corporate messaging and the absence of support actually comes back to the manager's discretion of flexibility. I can attest to the unsurprising nature of this truth; it is the reason my career as a leadership consultant focuses on the re-envisionment of modern-day management.

The parents who felt supported attributed that to their direct manager or their spouse's direct manager. About 15% of participants spoke on behalf of their partners' company and policies; the overall well-being was palatable when the husband or wife had an understanding superior, which is in stark contrast to those who did not. Participant Z shared, "My company acknowledged the risks of COVID, the impact it has on families, and offered employees resources. It made such a difference. We were fortunate because my husband's boss was also empathetic. Even though my husband's boss is married to a woman who is a stay-at-home mom and did not have to be interrupted by his children, he was tolerant of our situation. We could tell his attitude was influenced greatly by the company's expectations. A real blessing."

DEFAULT TO RESPONSIBILITY IS THE CORNERSTONE OF GENDER INEQUITY – THE INEQUITY THAT HAS PERMEATED OUR HOMES AND OFFICES AND REMAINED THERE, BILLOWING, GROWING IN BRAWN. AND NOW THAT IT IS EXPOSED, KNOWLEDGE AND UNITY COMPROMISE ITS LONGEVITY. IT IS TIME FOR EVICTION.

# IV: CULTURE AND UPBRINGING

We buy boys construction toys and buy girls baby dolls and homemaker sets. The conditioning begins when we take the first swallow of earthly oxygen. Just take a peek at Gabrielle Galimberti's *Toy Stories* exhibit if my statement seems too bold: The global norm is far from teaching children gender neutrality. But what happens when women, or men, step outside the predetermined gender boxes (and all the behaviors that come along with them)? How does this affect our professional and personal lives?

## CONFIDENCE: FROM CHILDHOOD TO THE WORKFORCE

We are the products of both nature and nurture. Psychologists repeatedly visit this debate ad nauseum – a true disquisition on how genetic inheritance and environmental factors shape human development. As an example, girls are more easily socialized than boys. Meaning, girls are adaptable in adjusting behavior that is considered acceptable to a particular society. Girls observe boys being reprimanded for rumbustious behavior at a young age and quickly adjust unruly practices. Our girls are praised for being "good," and continue down the path of people-pleasing and perfection-seeking. There is a repeated reward that we give our girls for this idealistic behavior, and that leads to girls being more cautious. As we know from Katty Kay and Claire Shipman, this caution decreases girls' likelihood to take risks and is directly correlated to resilience-building and confidence-creation. A decrease in risk-taking causes mistake aversion, and it is reported that girls find failure to be a reflection of their deeper qualities. Interestingly, resiliency derives from learning how to fail.

I think back to my childhood and the insistent need (and expectation) to be well-behaved and to not make mistakes – not only out of respect for my parents, but to prove that I was smart enough and capable enough (unsure which) to show the other kids (namely boys) how it is done. It is not outlandish to think that, in the developing brain of young girls, they think that being good will set them up for future successes. How disheartening that we now know the opposite to be true.

Life continues and girls evolve into women, boys into men. The years of women's efforts in education should now pay off, right? Turns out, confidence matters as much as competence in the workforce, and multiple studies show that women are less self-assured than men – another factor keeping women stuck in middle management and below. Women are recorded to not consider themselves as ready for promotions as their male counterparts, predict they will not do as well on tests, and they generally underestimate their abilities. Studies have been conducted to compare male and female intelligence and both genders score virtually the same in all subjects. However, if a woman is not required to answer a question, she will leave it blank for the fear of the answer being incorrect. According to the research, men do not suffer from this fear of failure; rather, they overestimate their abilities and performance, while women do the exact opposite. Is it probable men also overestimate their contribution to the household, just as they overestimate their abilities to perform? The data McKinsey collected about perceived workloads between men and women insinuates so.

In order to help women achieve more success in corporations, we must provide a way to practice confidence building – the very thing we took from our girls in adolescence. While potentially counterintuitive, the best way to build confidence is by failing – identifying the armor of resiliency in the process – and trying again. We need to create systems to appreciate women's aptitude and help women understand the seat at the table is theirs for the taking.

We know there are behaviors and actions that cause girls to hone the natural disposition of being easily socialized. This means active work is required to counter the damage that has been done – both in corporations and at home. Showing girls how to fail, be resilient, not give up, persevere, and even run amuck sometimes, will better prepare them for life. Women exhibiting confidence through their own behaviors is a starting point, and so too is fighting stereotypes within the home. Demonstrating capability to children in varying regards, such as careers, education, chores, and care is key to how children view the world – and ample amounts of nurture go into this.

## LA FAMILIA

In one example alone, it is clear to see why nature and nurture set a path for who we become as adults. The only other thing as powerful as our genetics is our family. The way we were raised, the overarching taboos and mores, religious affiliations, political stances, and the like, are ingrained into our being from day one.

At a young age, my father taught me how to hammer nails into the side addition of the house he was working on with my maternal grandfather. My grandfather taught me how to punch patterns into tin for the pie safe we were making for my mom. My parents taught me how to cook creatively, speak eloquently, clean thoughtfully, and mainly, taught me how to be self-sufficient. I observed the work my parents did and now know there were some gendered elements in their responsibility sets, but I was particularly fortunate to be in a home that was not so typical. My father cooked, cleaned, and my mother did yard work and home improvement projects. Gender roles, specifically what girls and boys should like and be like, were fuzzy to me. I found delight in playing with my Polly Pocket, but so too did I revel in watching the '94 Camaro SS swirl around my Hot Wheels loop and launch forward with a crash landing. I loved my dance classes and singing lessons but was a proud girl when reaching the summit of Mt. Washington at the age of 11. My predisposition was one of being like my mom and my dad. I intently listened to lessons about the world and my parents' experiences within it as I crafted what I wanted my life to look like. I learned relatively quickly that my experience – fighting gender normalities and embracing both my feminine and masculine qualities – was the exception, not the rule.

In my 66 interviews, only two women were responsible for taking out the trash and the recycling. The trash, car, and yard work were the three home items that were unequivocally the man's responsibility. How interesting that those three tasks do not require *being in the home*. Participant I stated that, "All schooling falls on moms for better or for worse. We are also responsible for laundry, cleaning, food prep, and the like because, well, men don't really know any better." I for one do not share these beliefs; but then again, I take out the trash in our household.

If women assume that men do not know any better, shame on us. I am fain to tell parents that we must inculcate our girls and boys about the ways of the world to course correct. Boys need to clean up their messes, and moms need to stop enabling them! Girls need to experience failure, and fathers must help girls see their worth is far beyond beauty! My father taught me to be bold, speak up, and fight like hell for justice. *I am working on it, dad.*

## SOCIETY'S JUDGEMENT

Whether it be *Vanity Fair*, *The Guardian*, or *National Geographic*, the discussion about gender roles, family expectations, and going against the grain is well-reported on and is of interest to the populous. Depending upon the reader, personal accounts may be met with judgement, relatability, or even relief. I have scoured these articles and the trend is lamely consistent: Whether a Mormon from Utah or a Muslim from Turkey, bearing children is an expectation for women.

When women choose to not embrace their capability to birth a child, they are met with condemnation and dismissiveness. It makes for a great article, but it is not a supreme way to live. "You're young, you'll change your mind" is the phrase I have heard too often. Perhaps it is the retrojection of what occurred to the statement giver (in my experience this comes from only women). When I probe further, some of the women recount their experiences. Having children was not an active choice; instead, it was an assumption, one sealed by the fate of fertility or the absence of birth control. It was "simply" something women did. There are accounts of women who feared vocalizing the questioning of procreation. No woman wants to be ostracized for being inquisitive or to be labeled as different when the assumption is that being different is a bad thing (do not listen to that, be different!). We all try a little too hard to not stir the patriarchal pot.

I have been fortunate to be in the presence of progressive thinkers. A reviewer of this publication and author of the Foreword, as well as a published author herself, Gloria Feldt, taught me (among other things) to think big, not to limit myself, and that if I think I cannot do something, I cannot. The opposite is true too. We all need to place value on mentorship and seeking out those from whom we can learn. I have also had my fair exposure to people who, regardless of their decent qualities, make a point to belittle and disregard my convictions and queries. To me, there are few lower blows.

It is evident – through research and my personal experience – that the American culture was mainly unable to accept the decision of women who did not want or need to be a mother. The repeated conditioning of what we all have been taught to think about women – what is expected and what is necessary – likely resulted in an abundant number of people on this earth. Women were fooled into thinking it was for them, or knew it was not for them all along and saw no way out. But that was then. In the present day we are facing a falling fertility rate; women like me are pondering optionality, risk, cost, and principle. Women with more education and newfound success at work (not to mention greater access to contraception) are deciding to remain childless.

It is the women who challenged the expectations of having children we have to thank for scratching at the itch of choice and the right to choose. It is also these women we have to thank for showing the world a woman's voice is not to be stifled, and that there is great power in a woman who resists, inspires, dissents, discovers, perseveres, and leads. But what if I told you all this wanting (or not wanting) children business is in fact directly correlated to a woman's ability to be successful in her career? After what I have shared in this text, is it any wonder? About 35% to 40% of women with lucrative careers that demand long hours and extensive education are childless. Twenty percent actually want children, but only five percent end up having a child. This leaves approximately 15% with no children, but a satisfying or prosperous career. Perhaps this is the underbelly of our lower fertility rate. Men, on the other hand, who want successful careers and have demanding long hours (and yes, extensive education), but who also want children, are left childless only three percent of the time. Yet again, we face the improbability of having it all when we are doing it by ourselves. There is a clear identification of the discordance when comparing women's lives to men's, both professionally and personally.

# MEDIA

I was flipping through the channels in early January 2021 when I came across an episode of *Full House* called "Girls will be boys." Intrigued, I remained there. Michelle, the youngest of the unorthodox San Francisco family and a queen of blarney, had plans to play with her male friend Teddy. Another boy, Aaron Bailey, interjected and told Teddy how playing with girls was stupid. Teddy talked Aaron into going to Michelle's house to play and a series of gendered events unfolded. The boys wanted to play "superheroes." Aaron declared that Michelle could not possibly play with them, since the only female superhero was Wonder Woman and, based on Michelle's blonde locks, that wasn't allowed. Aaron designated Michelle to act like Superman's mom; she could provide the boys with food for power. (Ah-hem, I'm pretty sure this Aaron character was not 6' 3" like Superman!)

Aaron displayed colors of distaste for Michelle and had all the characteristics of a bully; he was stereotypically machismo. He wanted to trivialize her, aggravate her, and was adamant that Teddy no longer play "house" with her or he would spread scuttlebutt about him liking girls' *interests* around school. This left Michelle wishing she were a boy so she could play not only with boys, but the games that boys were encouraged to play. This episode originally aired in 1992. The lesson of the show was to embrace differences, and it also demonstrated how bossy people are not the best option when picking friends. Not a bad message to convey, but it surely is not the take-away I had as an adult. The "good" and "bad" assignment to gender roles – not to mention the associated tasks – was perspicuous and quite frankly disappointing. I personally will be sure to forfend against any young minds being exposed to messages such as this, but herein lies the point...

In our most formative years, we are exposed to the media's portrayal of normal, parents' beliefs and biases, and, without correction, the pendulum of change does not swing very far. I am reminded of a boy whom I babysat for about a year when I was earning my undergraduate degree. He simply adored the Pink Power Ranger at the age of three. Two years later, I was asked to watch he and his two siblings for a parent's night out. I was eager to ask about the Pink Power Ranger and get a peek at his expansive memorabilia. Jack (pseudonym) was thunderstruck. "I NEVER liked the PINK Power Ranger," he insisted. "Pink is for GIRLS. It's the green one I like." I shot a look at his older brother who was approving of Jack's response. How sad, I thought. A simple joy of liking the Pink Power Ranger was stripped away because he, a boy, plainly was not supposed to like the color representative of femininity.

From laundry detergent to home cleaning agents, brands have placed women at the forefront. Concurrently, men are the face of grills, power washing agents, and tools. It was not until late 2019 that I saw brands making a concerted effort to include women in historically male tasks and vice versa. As an example, Tide created a series of ads where either both parents participated in the laundry or the dad was doing it solo. Lowes started to incorporate women into home improvement projects such as painting and remodeling. It is subtle, but it is progress.

# V: AN INDEPENDENT LIFE

As part of my research, I interviewed women who were single and childless to compare the male/female divide when removing the hefty responsibility of children. I reached saturation with this subset of interviewees after about 15 hours. A recurring theme was having feelings of loneliness and uncertainty. Some participants expressed fortune for being able to have additional personal time – something that was previously muted in a typical work week with commuting and social commitments. Most relevant, childless women did not feel disproportionately affected by the global pandemic, but were aptly aware their female colleagues were, and knew the hours were grueling. Participant R shares, "The children, particularly those who were not school-aged, seemed to be a heavier lift for moms alone, at least in my experience. There were no nannies, no daycares, and that left a screaming two-year-old – our new colleague, so to speak. You could see the strain on moms' faces during weekly calls. It was a mix of embarrassment and being overwhelmed."

Participant V recalls the primary change being an increase in weekly calls. "Prior to COVID, there may have been one call a week for a certain initiative, but all of the sudden there were three calls a week. Communication needed to increase, and therefore meetings increased; it was my company's way of staying connected. As the crisis became more familiar, calls decreased to adjust for the evolving reality." Childless interviewees who were in management quickly succumbed to long days. Participant C knew her colleagues were struggling (just as she was) and she would work actively to engage with her team after hours to maintain a personal connection. Some participants saw furloughs ensue, mass layoffs, and weakened financial states at their place of employment, causing pause and concern for the future. Participant C (and other managers) dedicated more hours not only to be available, but to be a voice of reason when fears emerged. For one participant, limited technical resourcing was a prevalent issue, and the company relied on employees to provide their own laptops and WiFi connections. It was not until seven months into the pandemic they were given company-owned computers. Adaptability was vital, and organizations relied on management to be composed and reassuring amidst the storm. More than one participant told me the company informed managers to be flexible with their teams, especially if the team members had children. However, this was not an official decree and was not tracked or measured for success. This meant each boss was a little different and could make the difference between making work tolerable during this time or forcing someone out.

Participant H1 works in HR and saw the disproportionate burden on women firsthand – whether the mother was on her team or not. "Mothers were always interrupted by their children, and in some cases the husband was nearby... Not even a flinch from one husband when a mom was holding a screaming toddler in her lap and also on a team meeting call. It was so disappointing to see." Participant H1 also supports a younger employee population and shared the focus was more on social disappointments and financial concern, not on burnout. One single participant contracted the virus several months into the pandemic. She recounts that period as "pretty distressing." She said it is not only hard to be sick, but it is hard to be sick and to receive no comfort or socialization whatsoever. Yet a married woman with two children, who also contracted the virus, was distressed for an entirely different set of reasons. Not only was she frighteningly ill, her spouse and two children were miserable. She would have brokered a deal with Hades to have been single and childless when she was sick. A reason for us all to count our blessings – the grass scarcely seems to be greener elsewhere.

Another interviewee, Participant I1 who is married and childless, shared that her career as an artist was turned upside down. From pending shows to exhibits, all her work was put on hold. She conveyed the level of disappointment was high, but it was not so dissimilar from her male colleagues. To support her business of being a skillful artist, she also works in education. She shared with me her (female) superior did an amazing job organizing different subsets of teams to assess risk and respond quickly. "With a good leader, this pandemic seems more tolerable, especially when I hear stories from my peers about their bosses." Childless women were transparent about the challenge of managing work stress, financial stress, and interpersonal stress if a partner was in the picture. They also sympathized for women with children, and all expressed a level of trepidation in envisioning what their life (a woman's life with children) must be like.

In an unexpected variable, Participants A1, X, and A – all childless – indicated an awareness of additional dog parent responsibilities, e.g., walks, feeding, and play, from the start of the pandemic. Each shared with me there was always a slight tilt of responsibility with dog care prior to the pandemic, but when stay-at-home orders ensued, the cumulative hours spent in the day caring for the dog increased exponentially. One woman told me it felt unprofessional to have a whimpering dog on her Zoom meetings; she was stressed to have to dulcify the pup, move him into another room, or reprimand him – especially when her husband was upstairs not being bothered or on calls. Participant X was one of many individuals who purchased (or adopted/fostered) a dog in 2020. She was getting little sleep each night, as any dog owner who has had a puppy can understand. Her partner's sleep was rarely interrupted. Could care for a dog act as a precursor to equitable care of children?

While this subset of participants did not feel disproportionately affected by COVID-19 compared with their childless male counterparts, there was a recognition of changes in communication, intensified feelings, and an increased energy output – especially for those who managed others or who worked with children in a virtual environment. And there was a compelling case for a childless woman's disproportionate amount of work relating to dog care.

# VI: PERSISTENT INEQUITIES

THE TRUE DISENFRANCHISED SEEK BELONGING.

THE WEAK SEEK POWER.

THE STRONG EMPOWER.

THE FEARLESS PERSEVERE.

THE APPREHENSIVE SOLICIT ALLIANCE.

THE JUST INVITE JUSTICE.

## INVISIBLE WORK AND RESPONSIBILITY REFUSAL

Multiple women who confided in me about their experiences during the pandemic shook their heads with bafflement when they mentioned invisible work. Participant D1 revealed, "It's called invisible for a reason. My husband does not seem to know how much I do behind the scenes, so to speak."

When stay at home orders were instated, outsourcing work became non-viable, at least for a period of time. Parents did not trust having another person – whether dedicated to childcare, meal prep, or house cleaning – in their home. A parent's reality shifted quickly; this work would still need to be done, but the luxury of having help was put on hold. The struggle with making this decision was consistent. In urban areas, the primary challenge was transportation; how does a person get a nanny or house cleaner to the home or apartment safely sans public transportation? In all locations, parents questioned service providers' fastidiousness with being cautious, wearing a mask, and social distancing. In suburban areas where childcare facilities opened back up more quickly, parents had another difficult decision to make: Were they putting their children at risk? I learned from participants it was a matrix of decisions, none with clear-cut answers.

Participant U shared with me that she had someone coming to clean her house for years, admitting bashfully that both she and her partner had not scrubbed a toilet or vacuumed in quite some time. As the virus made its debut, she and her husband knew it was unwise to have the person who cleaned for them in their home. "We had to start cleaning – or should I say I did. Mopping, cleaning the bathrooms, dusting... all of it." Participant U told me that arguments ensued when it came to the new responsibility of who was going to clean. She was fatigued by the disagreements, and also knew home cleanliness in a time of a global health crisis was indispensable. She assumed the responsibility alone.

Another woman, Participant C1, had a similar experience in that she opted to take on more work in order to spare her from circuitous arguments with her husband. "From helping my child with schoolwork, to spending the day on Sundays prepping food for the week, to doing appreciably more laundry, daily cleaning, maintaining my full-time job, grocery shopping, and coming up with activities to keep my children active, I physically do not have an ounce left in me – ever, it seems." I captured the feeling of exasperation that Participant C1 and others experienced when speaking about their spouses and the attitudes with which they were met. Some husbands would complain so tediously the participants decided the only way to make the home less miserable for themselves and for their children was if they did the majority of home and childcare work, embedding the idea of who is responsible for invisible work more deeply into the makeup of the family unit. Our children are watching the *default to responsibility*.

In April 2020, the early innings of the pandemic, divorce interest and agreement increased by 39%. Now that we have reached the pandemic's one-year anniversary, I anticipate marriage rates are continuing to unravel at the seams. It is no wonder people are noticing their spouses' flaws at a new scale. There are multiple reasons working from home can uncover incompatibility. From needing to share a table with someone for eight to 10 hours a day to trying to hear a colleague over a partner's soniferous voice (my husband was voted "loudest voice in the crowd" in high school), it is no question the dynamics of working from home and sharing space is difficult. But is it not more challenging to comprehend how something as elementary and straightforward as dividing invisible work cannot be resolved? The tension output cuts a sharp line in the sand of resistance. My guess? Gender equity has the power to decrease divorce rates, too.

Twelve percent of my participants who had children were either divorced or never married. These mothers are solely responsible for invisible work, and in most cases, are not outsourcing monotonous but necessary tasks. In speaking with these mothers, who literally do everything for their child or children and for themselves, I could not help but realize how much it sounded like a married woman's experience. Laundry, dishes, cooking, cleaning, childcare, schedule management, necessity shopping, schoolwork support... the list goes on. The primary differences for non-married women with children? First, a double whammy regarding household income – one less annual salary and a lower take-home amount than her male counterparts. And second, there were no arguments to be had about sharing labor.

I am not saying being a lone parent to a child or children is desirable, but I am saying the sufficient examples of poor attitudes from male spouses toward matters of additional responsibility – in the home and with children – may be a contributing factor to the recent increase in divorce rates.

## ASKING FOR HELP

If we consider our car care analogy, the person who owns the car is ultimately responsible. Is this perhaps what occurs when we think about *default to responsibility* and the associated demands that go along with it? Ninety-five percent of participants informed me that if they needed help, they had to *ask their husbands*. The husband's default was to only assist when asked explicitly or when it came time for a family meeting. Participant F was a voice for seven of her co-interviewees. "After two or so months of the global pandemic, I thought I may be nearing wit's end. I was rising early to prepare three meals for the day, transitioning directly to schooling for my children for about an hour, and then slid right into a full day's work, which was simultaneously filled with child interruptions. Once dinner was served, I had three times the dishes and laundry to do before getting back to my paid work. I had to sit my husband down and ask for help." In some cases, the result of a heart-to-heart discussion was the adoption of multiple tasks that were previously not considered to be a husband's job. These included changing cat litter, taking the dog out, going grocery shopping, assuming responsibility for one meal a day (which tended to be breakfast), and taking turns on more tasks than previously.

I fear that a woman's felt responsibility, along with the enablement of care (e.g., maternity leave, and the default to caring for and providing for something she feels she owns), ensures that women take on more than their fair share. Without awareness about women's likelihood to not ask and just do regarding childcare, organization, cleanliness, health, and the like, it will continue; and if we want to reach equity, that needs to change. Discussing equality in the home sounds daunting to some. The women I interviewed told me it was never a pleasant topic to raise, and except for several outliers, husbands were dismayed. Some felt terrible for not knowing what their wives were experiencing, and others recognized the stark unevenness of the playing field. Interestingly, every interviewee framed the additional help as just that – *help*. The woman was still taking ownership for the overarching cloud of responsibility, instead of placing ownership on her spouse. When women face this reality, they need to have the courage to raise the issue of who is responsible for what.

Similarly, men must stop to consider how time is spent and meet their partners half-way. While I am not pretending to be a qualified party for marital advice, I feel strongly that dividing responsibilities in the home will lead to less resentment, frustration, and miscommunication. Help should relate to a person doing something that is temporary. A woman may help do the laundry once and awhile when it is the man's job. A man may help water the plants occasionally even if it is the woman's job. That is what help is – assistance. Changing the rhetoric around responsibility and ownership of unpaid work is a crucial part of how we climb the equitability mountain.

## EARNING

As of September 2020, women in the United States earned 83 cents on the man's dollar. Upon reflection, I am encouraged to see cent by cent increases, but perhaps that is a dismal statement. It is quite discouraging to know that the wage gap exceeds $10,000 annually when looking at women's and men's median salaries – a $300,000 deficit for women over their careers. We continue to see the consequence of pay inequity that was established many years before. What's more, the gap is greater when assessing women of color. Latinas earn only 55 cents for every dollar paid to white, non-Hispanic men, while Black women earn just 63 cents on that dollar. The inequities persist.

In my research, I found that 75% of married participants in urban areas make a negligible amount of money compared to their spouses. However, I also discovered that 85% of married participants who live in rural geographic locations earn more – up to double – of what their husbands earn. This finding is complementary to recent research. In the United States, women who have children under the age of 18 reportedly earn more than their husbands. This said, the wage gap exists regardless of industry and regardless of education level. Mothers earning more than their spouses is true for 74% of Black mothers, 47% of Latina mothers, and 45% of white mothers. The takeaway: For "like jobs," women are underpaid compared to their male counterparts. But within households (and with disparate jobs), women frequently outearn their spouses.

The ripple effect of women being forced out of their careers based on the COVID-19 pandemic is profound and will have severe economic implications – compounded by the long withstanding gremlin of pay inequity.

The interconnectivity among women's inequitable pay, disproportionate home care, and child rearing capabilities is transpicuous. Corporations cannot stand idly by as women wait for legislation to be passed for equal pay. Companies have an opportunity to stimulate the economy, reduce poverty, and inject security into civilization; but instead, they have done little to assure psychological and financial safety.

Eighty percent of the participants that I interviewed shared an eerily similar dialogue about company expectations and the associated dissonance of their conveyed support. The universal expectation was to continue at the same level of quantity output and expertise. Additionally, the economic factors for those in sales professions were not seriously considered. Predictions were reworked for quarterly company profits, but individual goals and key performance indicators (KPIs) went forth unadjusted. And now? Women are facing poor performance reviews and as a consequence not earning their annual raises, bonuses, and associated variable compensation.

Participant L1 received a negative performance review in July of 2020 for the previous year. Three months of the year, she was on maternity leave caring for her child – solo. Five months of the year, she had no childcare help at home due to the global pandemic. With this negative performance review came the justification for no annual increase, not even for cost of living. "I realize I was on maternity leave for some of this time, but that was before the pandemic hit. Why should I be penalized for caring for my infant? I understand the post-COVID reality with a baby at home made for shorter days, strange hours, and inconvenience, but the absence of consideration from my employer was crushing to me. And then to be made out to be a lazy or inadequate employee during my performance review in the hardest year of my life? Talk about a low point."

I would argue some companies took advantage of the fact their employees' attention was diverted and were able to capitalize on their assured failure. Perhaps draconian in nature, but where there is smoke, there is fire. The repetitive nature of similar circumstances leads me to believe it was a company's way to be guileful and opportunistic. At its best, the people governing organizations were oblivious to the additional layers of emotional exhaustion. At its worst, companies and the leaders within knew underperformance was a given for some employees – notably ones with children – more notably females with children – and would thereby see savings in regard to discretionary compensation. Another hit to women's pockets.

What corporations must realize is that the productivity being lost by women is not being made up by men. Long-term profits will suffer (consider replacement costs alone) without corporate support of women.

## BLACK LIVES MATTER

Black women face more barriers in organizational advancement than most other employees. Furthermore, the impact of COVID-19 on the Black community has been stark. The CDC records death rates of Black individuals to white individuals at almost a multiple of three. The emotional weight of not only the double shift seen by all participants in my study, but of racial violence and repeated injustice is inordinate.

Participants' eyes were not closed during the grotesque treatment toward people of color across the country. When the topic of social justice came up in my interviews – and it did for about 50% of the participants that elected to do so – I felt the fear and sadness in some of the participants' eyes as they considered the fundamental biases and political factors at play. There was a unanimous agreement among participants who raised the subject of social justice that having discussions with their children about what was going on in the country was onerous, but necessary. One participant, F1, shared, "It is moments of unrest that create virtuous futures. But we are smack in the middle of unrest."

# "AND SO WE LIFT OUR GAZE, NOT TO WHAT STANDS BETWEEN US, BUT WHAT STANDS BEFORE US..."
## - AMANDA GORMAN

Several Black participants were willing to edify me about how this heavy weight they carry – an absence of care, a daily concern for safety, a gnawing inkling they are underpaid, and warding off daily censorious glares – is nothing new. Consistent disappointment and loss are what to expect.

Prior to the COVID-19 pandemic, unemployment in the United States among Black individuals was slightly more than three percent higher than white people. As the outbreak enlarged, the unemployment disparity continued. The long-term repercussions of segregation contribute to denying Black Americans jobs, salaries, and health. On the journey to women's equitability, we must challenge all inequities and injustices along the way. We must be a voice for our fellow women in totality.

Participant E1 was responsible for schooling her children at home at the onset of the pandemic and is still teaching them from home in 2021. The son is old enough to ask questions about what he sees or hears on the television, and a conversation that was relevant daily in her household was that Black Lives Matter. "My son, the eldest, could not reconcile why a case has to be made for the validity of his life. He would look at his two sisters, eyes swelling, wanting to know why he – why they – were different." Participant E1 informed me it was a daily struggle to educate her son about the injustices of this world and the hate-filled history of the nation. This participant told me her experience was no different from friends with children at similar ages. The hard facts about racism were a new dinnertime conversation. "The physical, psychological, and emotional energy it demands from mothers like me, to explain the atrocities of our time and times past, is nothing I wish upon anyone. But I know with efforts like these, and unification, my son will see change in his lifetime."

## A SEA OF EMOTIONS

The ambit of emotional effects as a result of the pandemic pertaining to sickness, isolation, and all of the changes that proceeded, are vast. My interviewees spoke about not only their experiences in the home but opened up about their emotional well-being, as well.

Participant E told me, "I feel like I am not doing any of it very well. I do not know how it is remotely possible to be a teacher for my children, to care for them, and to also manage – not to mention excel – in my career. The whole reason businesses have offices is for the purpose of getting away from distractions... And we are now in environments with only distractions. All the while I'm concerned about my performance, my pay, and my future trajectory. I feel bad for leaving my children in front of the television, I have guilt for being less patient. I do not feel good at anything."

The above quote summarizes an aspect of how multiple interviewees felt. In fact, 60% of women with children said some version of those same words, "I do not feel good at anything right now." They revealed a complete removal of self-care, a staggering amount of sustained stress, and the disappointment they felt daily about how competent they were at any given thing. As we already know, women's conditioning to be a perfectionist and to seek approval makes the hit even harder. When a person is pulled in more directions than thought possible, there is not a lot of room for feeling balanced or for recognizing self-accomplishment. To add to the intricacy, studies using fMRI scans have found that women tend to activate their amygdalae more easily in response to negative emotional stimuli than men do. What this means is women are more likely than men to create memories of negative events and are more prone to ruminate about what went wrong.

In the effort to get women back into the workplace – or to remain within it – we must be aware that women are predisposed to quickly and easily recalling moments of perceived inadequacy, either at home or at work. Disabling a woman from achieving, by placing more responsibility on her and less on a spouse, will sustain the feelings of self-doubt and will contribute to increased levels of anxiety and depression. Women, and most of whom I spoke with, face a challenge ahead in acknowledging it is not their deficiency as professionals or mothers, but is the paucity of resources offered to both working fathers and mothers.

## "MANAGING WORK, DOING WELL AT WORK, AND NOT BEING A BAD PARENT...IT'S A LOT."
### -PARTICIPANT K1

Just as COVID-19 has worn on the emotional resilience of mothers, LGBTQ+ women are almost twice as likely as people overall to cite mental health as one of the biggest challenges during COVID-19. There will be a lingering aftermath from this pandemic – specifically with women and LGBTQ+ women. Creating resources for applicable coteries will expedite recovery. Time is of the essence.

Participant H shared an experience that was telling of the nature of quarantine for working parents. She recounted a moment when she was on a video call with colleagues and an uproarious child tore into the room. "My colleague, a working mother, paused. Pure dread corroded her otherwise relaxed face. The child catapulted himself toward the computer – specifically the camera I think, as if it's the missing engine to his train set. The noise doesn't let up and my colleague gives us a shrug – signaling that she will be back. We adjust our focus and continue on. At that moment I envisioned her tenacious son, pleading for play, while my colleague petitions for him to go elsewhere."

It is undoubtedly peculiar to see a toddler stealth bomb a meeting. But 95% of interviewed participants had an experience with colleagues' children being a part of weekly meetings. Some individuals snicker and take a light-hearted approach to the preposterous reality the pandemic has shaped. Others disengage, annoyed with the decrease in production, oblivious to the stress the parent is feeling.

Participant H's description is likely to cause some discomfort. All of us have experienced some level of her recount. If we put ourselves in the parent's shoes or even in the shoes of the colleagues, we may experience frustration, concern, or angst. But what this participant's recall really showed me is that the level of stress endured by mothers was sustained – for months. This was not the once-a-year abnormal occurrence. This was a daily struggle, for all parties involved.

# VII: A RELIANT LIFE

The data paints a clear picture of adults' experiences during the global pandemic – both for those married and single, with children and without. But what about children's perspectives? How do parents think their children are managing the changes instituted because of the coronavirus?

There is no question that mental health concerns have skyrocketed. Dr. Adrian James, United Kingdom's leading psychiatrist, believes the aftermath of COVID-19 is the greatest psychological challenge since the second world war. In fact, 1.5 million children need additional or new psychiatric attention as a result of the pandemic.

Parents divulged the fears they had for their children. Participant M1 recounts the deterioration of her son as the months progressed. Early in the pandemic, all school doors were closed, and virtual learning was implemented in an immediate and impromptu way. School districts were trying to adapt and continue children's education amidst an overwhelmingly uncertain time. Participant M1 told me her son did not find it to be so bad at first. The uncertainty and absence of regular school was somewhat exciting – reminiscent of a break, almost. But that sheen quickly faded from her son's perspective. He became tired of sitting behind a computer, and summer break could not have come fast enough. When Participant M1's son commenced school again in the fall of 2020, the school was operating on a hybrid model. The pairing allowed her son to get some social interaction, which seemed to keep his anxiety at bay. But as they entered the end of the 2020 year, and in-person days became far less frequent as COVID-19 infection rates soared, her son's behavior took a turn for the worse. "He would simply drop to the ground and sob if he didn't get his way, over the smallest of issues. My husband and I set up a treadmill to try to help him learn remotely but stay more active. We feared the absence of socialization and far fewer steps per day – not to mention play – seemed to be making him more reactive and less emotionally mature." In gathering data from mothers, I recognized a broad-spread feeling; parents knew they needed to approach their children of all ages with mansuetude as they navigated these uncharted waters.

Other participants' struggles with their children ranged in variation and complexity. Multiple children were classified as gifted and had Individualized Education Plans (IEP) for learning. Participant F1, who has two daughters, informed me of the added pressure she felt in her attempt to customize her children's learning. One of her children becomes easily bored – always eager to rush through tasks. She felt her daughter responded particularly poorly to her when she offered instructions, specifically pertaining to schooling. Participant F1 surmised that it is the mother-daughter or parent-child dynamic that makes it more difficult. "Children are taught to respect and to listen to their teachers... It's not that they aren't taught to behave a certain way with parents, but when a parent becomes the teacher, the family dynamics shift. It's unfamiliar and it seems unfavorable."

An additional obstacle for parents whose children received support with learning or were on customized plans, was the reduction of this assistance. It was difficult for teachers to assign more complex work to children in gifted programs. When I asked parents why they thought this was, they pointed to the obvious: Burnout. Teachers were learning not only how to teach kids virtually, but they were unfamiliar in some cases with the technical tools themselves. There was consensus that individual attention in the classroom dissipates when behind a screen. Fifty percent of those interviewed with school-aged children specifically mentioned the perceived decrease in 1:1 attention. According to Participant F2, "A lot of these teachers were using their personal cell phones for parent-teacher calls and had to purchase a second monitor. I think the screen is inconducive to learning for younger kids… And the ability to focus on kids more personally is removed."

Participant O2's child was in the third grade and was being assigned fifth and sixth grade math prior to stay-at-home orders. As sickness spread and teachers pivoted to a remote-only teaching environment, the personalization became sparse. Participant O2, among others, did not want her child to suffer educationally because of an absence of structured school, fewer challenging assignments, and individual attention. The holus-bolus onslaught of the pandemic came to life as parents described the pairing of inflated responsibility and emotional exertion.

Thirty-five percent of parents shared with me that schooling in the spring of 2020 was a free for all. Attendance was not consistently taken, school hours were loose or cut short, and homework was arguably minimal. It was not until the autumn of 2020 that schools had plans in place for a better delivery of education – including expectations for online learning.

Some of those expectations required children to stay seated, hour after hour, or risk being marked as absent.

Participant G had the option of keeping her children home in September 2020 or sending them into the school building. She felt both options had downfalls. She did not feel it was wise for her children to return to school based on the evolving flow of information about COVID-19 and its risks; however, she did not want her children to feel isolated either. She opted to keep her children remote and was asked to pick up textbooks and other pertinent information for her children's school year. "It was at that moment, as I walked through the school halls to get my children's schooling materials, I realized I made the correct decision. My children's elementary school is old... The infrastructure is questionable, and I have no doubt there's poor ventilation. Even as I picked up the items for my kids, I was ready to get out of there."

Participant N1, an essential worker and mother of three, had little interest in recalling the spring of 2020. Her youngest daughter had always struggled with academics, but when the social aspect was taken away, the daughter seemingly lost all her resilience. Every day was a screaming or crying match. "As a mother, and a working mother at that, getting my daughter to do her schoolwork and helping her accomplish daily tasks was one of the harder moments in my life. It was ripping a Band-Aid off on repeat."

Other challenges revolved around social pressures. Participant B2 knew her children wanted to play with other kids when schools, preschools, and childcare facilities were closed or operating with reduced hours, but she also knew that with more interaction the chances of exposure increased. She observed some parents creating small circles of friends – they were all in it together. She also experienced retaliating parents. A teenager contracted the virus and was involved in a school sport. "Some parents were annoyed that my friend told the school and the coach that her child got sick because it was 'taking the sport from the kids.' Really? She just protected all of those families… And it sounds like the children aren't being particularly friendly to the boy who got sick. Talk about additional stress no one needs."

Participant D told me her daughter has always been outgoing, but with the removal of daycare and an increase in television, as a necessity, she worries. She has a newfound appreciation for those who are childcare providers. "It's an acquired skill to entertain children in a healthful way. When there's nowhere to go and you do not want your kids to be couch potatoes, you have to get creative. And it's hard." Twenty-five percent of participants shared that their concerted nisus to keep their children engaged and active was tiring, and never seemed to be enough.

The full extent of the coronavirus's effect on mental health, especially for children, is yet to be seen and it is necessary for additional research to take place. But one thing is for certain, parents – both mothers and fathers – worry for the social and emotional impairments their children may face.

# VIII: WHERE WE GO FROM HERE

I read an extensive amount of secondary research for this project (six books, 35 articles, and seven academic journal publications). Consulting firms and media outlets offered a flurry of data around unemployment, illness rates, and women's experiences, all of which added substance to my research and supported my findings. I wanted to understand the subitaneous implications of the pandemic on people, mainly women, and determine the obstacles that stand before us. The journey led me to consider historical context and the shaping of the nation – all of which is relevant to why the global pandemic has wounded women so badly. The findings from my research are not anomalous. What this tells me is we are effective in reporting on and about a crisis, but the area most needing attention is how we recover. Knowing the issues and taking action to keep history from repeating itself are two distinct things.

## REACHING RECOVERY

The Gestalt perspective would pull upon socioeconomic factors, historical considerations, political influences, long-standing biases, psychological development, and cultural mores. In my attempt to do just that, I have never had more clarity. Women are indeed representative of the stifled engine, forced to run amidst chill and heat without the necessary parts that allow it to carry onward efficiently.

I meticulously reviewed my interview notes to propose how we support women, parents, and families. My findings metamorphosed from a chauvinism issue to a corporate culture one. The chicken or the egg, I know, but one has to take the lead, acting as an influential power to all constituents.

There are actions people – you, your partner, and the company for which you work – can take to change the prison of *default to responsibility*, and I will be leading this charge as a function of my company's offerings and mission. To manage crises well, companies must prepare adequately. It just so happens that crisis preparation has everything to do with systematic support for families, which will aid organizations in crisis recovery. To get on the road to recovery, there are solutions to widespread problems that can be readily enacted.

## SOLUTIONS TO IMPLEMENT:

### Gender Equity Steering Committee (GESC)

At each corporation, a steering committee should be erected. The group should be charged with assessing equity concerns and making observations of inequities. In partnering with HR, the Steering Committee Chair will have access to demographic and salary information. The Chair will also be empowered with decision-making autonomy to support the efforts and vision of the GESC, taking the committee's considerations and concerns and turning the ideologies into actionable, company-wide changes.

Employee feedback should be sought to prioritize needs. For example, women in the United States consider equal pay a top workplace issue. It is necessary to pair employee findings with revised recruitment and hiring efforts, as well as behavioral standards and pay scale adjustments.

The Steering Committee should be a diverse set of individuals, modeling the indispensability of multifariousness. Communication to the organization about equality efforts, and challenges, should stem from this cohort, including company-wide and company-sponsored guest speakers.

Each organization should have a GESC and should also encourage the creation of employee resource groups (ERGs) for additional engagement and discourse.

Nuances of corporate dealings must be considered, e.g., budgets, profit modeling, board review, and multi-phase rollouts for advancements.
The GESC will need to receive unconscious bias training to best serve as equality reformers.

## Evaluation of Benefits

It is encouraged for HR teams to do an audit on all benefits, evaluating cost to value. The benefits under immediate review should include parental leave policies and health benefits. A multi-phased approach will likely be necessary based on workforce expenditures. While coverage of in vitro fertilization may take time to incorporate into health benefits, as an example, it is of paramount importance to rework parental leave.

The first correction is to match the paternity leave to the existing maternity leave. In the United States, the average paid leave for a woman is 4.1 weeks. At a minimum, men must be afforded the equivalency in paid leave for paternity care. Although men and women are eligible for 12 weeks of unpaid leave via FMLA when welcoming a child, the *unpaid* aspect ensures the impracticality for both parents – and one at that – of utilizing the FMLA policy.

Another highly desirable consideration is a monthly stimulus check provided to childcare providers for families who have children. This ensures women's return to work and normalizes a new way of how we think about childcare and equitability.

## *Training:*

Management Training -- Whether virtual or not, being an effective manager means more than measuring KPIs and being a task master. Managers must learn to lead and build cohesion within their teams. Almost 60% of employees leave their place of employment due to their managers. The revolving door of recruitment, onboarding, and departures, costs companies six to nine months of an individual's salary. It adds up. During a crisis, employers need to do more to engage their employees, and that is where empathetic and efficacious management comes in. The influence of supportive management is pronounced and has high impact: Fifty eight percent of employees wish management would normalize empathy. Further, virtual management brings with it new obstacles. Prepare managers to communicate thoughtfully, frequently, and be present for their respective teams.

Trauma Informed Education -- As mental health continues to be a concern, with the worst effects to be demonstrated in the coming months, understanding trauma and how to manage those exposed to trauma – such as PTSD as a result of losing family members and extreme levels of stress caused by *default to responsibility* – are of new importance. A professional peer of mine, Mikhala Lantz-Simmons, a director of marketing at a professional services firm based in Montreal who holds a master's degree from the Center for Justice and Peacebuilding, is a state-certified mediator. She defines a trauma-informed organization as a company that:

- Has staff who has received training in trauma and that knows how to identify signs of trauma. Staff incorporates a trauma-informed framework into their interactions with others, meaning that they understand that people have stories and deserve to be treated with compassion and respect;

- Creates structures so that staff can practice meaningful self-care;

- Opens space for members of the organization, institution, or business to speak about stress;

- Fosters a sincerely relational environment where everyone's dignity is respected;

- Provides resources for getting help for those who need it.

## Revisit Organizational Policies

From family obligations to crisis management, revisiting policies that are created to maintain order and structure need to be evaluated. Considerations for organizations to improve employee support include but are not limited to flexible working hours, adjusted working hours, and increased leave. In one study with approximately 1200 full-time employees, almost half of those interviewed desired family leave and flexible hours far more than pay raises and amenities. This makes the case for the cost to value computation and gathering employee opinion. Spend money where it matters – on equality-driving factors.

## Crisis Preparation + Crisis Recovery (CPCR)

Revisiting organizational policies, as discussed in the previous bullet point, is a part of CPCR. Without understanding an internal model for corporate flexibility, crises will bring forth comparable amounts of ambiguity (and wreak havoc on families) as was seen with COVID-19. An internal model is in fact where to begin. Corporations that want to commit to equality and also retain talent will abide by a CPCR construct.

A corporate climate assessment, I call my offering the Thermometer Principle, is the foundation of understanding pressure points and factors of corporate weakness. This is the precursor to creating an internal reference for CPCR. It takes a detailed review of both the qualitative and quantitative, polling employees for candid sentiments, fears, and potential opportunities. Understanding recruitment standards, onboarding processes, continued enablement, organizational benefits, diversity efforts, and cultural norms within corporations, goes into crafting a CPCR guidebook. It is the amalgamation of an organization's practices and standards that make up how a company is likely to respond to crises. With concerted efforts to plan for the unexpected and consider how it will affect varying coteries within the company, the organization can adequately prepare and recover from crises – both at an individual level and a broader scale.

A combination of employee engagement tools and consultative services can support the efforts of CPCR and protect against unnecessary departures while increasing employee engagement and contentment. This ultimately saves organizations costly expenditures that derive from disengagement and turnover.

## Offer Solutions

I have demonstrated that gender equality is a business problem, and the aforementioned solutions will hit the bullseye of the target, fast-tracking the influence of equitability. What's more, corporations should be bold in their efforts; not only considering innovative solutions within the workplace to age-old problems, but also rallying behind individuals who want to challenge ineradicable beliefs. Offer employees who are parents a platform for discussing equity, division of labor, and the value of time, affording an opportunity for all to see through a different lens and the latitude to experience metanoia. Make less space for the privileged and encourage the privileged to make more space for the underrepresented.

## THE SPREADSHEET SOLVE: A MODEL FOR EQUITABLE PARENTING

There was a moment in my research when I was optimistic. Yes, after about 50 hours of interviews I had but one blithesome moment when a participant went into detail about how she and her husband managed the pandemic. I recommend their method as a guide for what parents should immediately consider as they strive to alter the oppressive present.

When childcare was obsolete during the first peak of the pandemic, a participant informed me that both she and her husband took care of their children in lieu of anyone else. They were afforded some flexibility to take turns with domestic work and childcare due to the combination of his family leave and hers. The couple made a spreadsheet that she told me was detailed and lengthy. They created shifts and correlated responsibilities within those shifts. In order for this couple to both participate in parenting and also be effective in their jobs, they agreed to a minimum of two-hour shifts. This allowed meaningful and uninterrupted work to be accomplished while the other individual was on "house and children duty."

The domestic responsibilities were bundled into the assigned time blocks. While reportedly only nine percent of husbands assume primary responsibility for meal preparation, this was not the case for the "Spreadsheet Solve" couple. There was no dodging gendered tasks. This participant's husband handled dinner duty almost each evening, and that also coincided with preparing the children for bed. While my interviewee was deputed to different shifts and comparable responsibilities, she acknowledged that her husband's evening shift was a difficult one – and it is one that 70% of my participants with children managed on their own, without recognition from their spouse about its demanding nature.

In addition to the programs in place at both employers which allowed this couple to take time when needed for family responsibilities and wellness days, both organizations also implemented a policy to allow for flexible working and block scheduling as a result of COVID-19. My participant and her husband used the spreadsheet as a visual representation for how time was allocated; the numbers and slots on the excel document did not discriminate. One person's time was not invaluable; instead, it was a beautifully simple way to divide responsibility fairly. The couple's earnings and approximate hourly wages were not written in a key; money did not dictate who carried more or less of the burden. The document enabled accountability and safeguarded against *default to responsibility*. The "divide and conquer" methodology is what partnership should be all about, is it not? This lulu of how to parent thoughtfully and combat inequality is deeply intertwined with the standards of the respective individuals' organizations. The way to institute change for a less ignorant and equitable future is the pairing of purposeful efforts in the home with intentional at-work policies. Not using a spreadsheet? It's time.

## BE PART OF THE (R)EVOLUTION

One of the more discouraging comments I heard from an interviewee was about an embedded belief of her own. She shared there was no official communication from her employer about COVID-19 (not unlike others) and also no variation of that communication to employees who had children. And that is not the depressing part. She continued to say that the industry she worked in is male-dominated due to the nature of the work itself. Since the majority are men, communicating a plan or any sentiments of support from an employer to their employees seemed to be a moot effort. The tone of the conversation was that since the audience was male, why would an employer need to offer flexibility? "They wouldn't need it," were her words.

The perception – even by women – is that women are the people who need extra allowances or support, because it is assumed from a corporate level that it is women who will need to pick up the pieces of childcare. Because, well, men cannot (will not?) do any of the childcare anyway. Disheartening! This is the precise example of what is keeping women out of the board room, out of the c-suite, and is pushing women out of the workforce all together.

What really hit me was this: Rather than demanding better of our men, starting with equity and divisions of labor, we retract to a simple (even though it is not so simple) state and justify the behavior of our spouses along the way. To think about a man taking primary responsibility for kids or for schooling, or even for house care, was a seemingly difficult concept for 30% of the participants (with children). It did not enter their ecosystem of consideration. "Why would he take responsibility for something that isn't his?" was the subtle but nagging susurrus buzzing around in my mind.

Women reading this text may have been nodding along at certain clauses or sighing a sigh of distress here and there. But now is the time to act on those emotions, not tuck them back in an undisclosed location to not be found again. Without conflict – the push and pull dynamic of negotiation – change gets stuck, almost like a die that stops short of its destination. But with conflict, the seed of an idea is planted, and with persistence that idea becomes less obscure, less bewildering. It becomes acceptable, even accepted. What is avant-garde in one decade is adopted to standard in the next. And with persistence, conflict, and steadfast acknowledgement of truth, we will reach equality.

# ESCHEW IGNORANCE, PURSUE TRUTH.

# DEMOGRAPHICS AND LIMITATIONS

## DEMOGRAPHICS:

There were 66 female participants with an average age of 35. One hundred percent of participants have a minimum of a four-year degree and 96% of the participants are employed. Any unemployment is a temporary result of COVID-19 layoffs. Participants are from nine states, including states in four time zones: PST, MST, CST, and EST. This study includes participants from two countries, the United Kingdom and the United States. Seventy-three percent of participants are married, six percent are divorced with children, 12% are single without children, three percent are separated without children, and six percent are never married with children. Six percent of the married population do not have children.

Eighty-eight percent of participants were from dual earning households. One hundred percent of the married and divorced participants are heterosexual and are classified as middle or upper class. One hundred percent of the participants were able to do their jobs from home.

The participants were three percent Latina, nine percent African American or Black, 15% South Asian or East Asian, 70% white, and three percent Pacific Islander.

The purpose of this research was to understand how the COVID-19 pandemic is affecting women's equality, including earning potential. Further, participants were told that the research will provide more detail about how women are affected during crises, notably the COVID-19 pandemic and that a goal of this research is to offer recommendations to corporations and families about how to achieve gender parity. Participants were required to acknowledge and sign an informed consent form. All participants who agreed to be a part of this study were interviewed about their experience. All personal information was kept confidential. I informed participants that taking part in this study was completely voluntary and that they had the right to refuse to participate or withdraw from participation at any time.

## LIMITATIONS:

Limitations for this study include an unequal representation of female minorities. Although variance of age, location, and profession was achieved, there is a need to produce a study where the majority of participants are not white. The gravity of the disproportionate work and associated consequences will likely vary with greater swings in socioeconomic levels. While it was my aim to demonstrate systemic inequities throughout this text, understanding nuanced accounts will offer a new level of insight, specifically with a more diverse sample set. I leveraged a snowball method to reach participants, and the scope of my reach and access to a broad set of women with diverse backgrounds was limited. Further research focusing on more diverse populations is needed.

An additional uncontrollable methodological limitation is the limits of self-reported data. While participants proactively agreed to participate, I must acknowledge that I am assuming responses and information provided to me were honest and forthcoming. This assumption is a possible limitation.

All married and divorced participants with children and without were heterosexual. Thus, an additional study is necessary to understand equality in same-sex households, with and without children. Men were not a part of this study and therefore it is important to also pursue an understanding of the male's perspective as it pertains to equality within the house and with childcare.

My potential bias must be recorded. I anticipated that I would find a worsened condition for women's lives based on the COVID-19 pandemic and the surrounding issues that ensued, including stay at home orders, closed schools, and childcare, as well as inflated home care needs. While I am a life-long advocate for women and a skeptic of men's contribution to tasks that have become or remained gendered, advocacy remains separate from empirical findings. However, my findings demonstrate and confirm an unequivocal conclusion about the increase of workload for women who have children and that there is a necessity for solution seeking. It is my commitment that I reported upon all interview notes and observations truthfully. My primary finding is that women are disproportionately affected during crises. CPCR must be instituted within organizations and *default to responsibility* must be recognized by corporations and within the home to reach gender parity.

# ABOUT THE AUTHOR

Brielle Valle is the owner of Brielle Valle Consulting (BVC), a leadership consulting firm that has one focus: Educating managers to achieve a cohesive and equitable culture. BVC offers women's equity programming for corporations, empowering women with knowledge on how to carry confidence, harness power, and take action for equality. Valle has 15 years of experience in Corporate Development and People Operations. She holds a B.S. in Speech Communication from Millersville University, an M.S. in Leadership and Organizational Communication from Northeastern University, is Predictive Index certified, has earned 40 credits toward a doctorate degree in Business Leadership from Walden University, and is currently earning a Diversity and Inclusion certificate from Cornell University. She has published works in SAGE Publications Ltd., Information Age Publishing, and Pearson. Her recent research aims to support corporations in reaching equality through understanding crisis preparation and crisis recovery.

Valle is open to additional research and publishing opportunities as well as collaboration inquiries, joint media efforts, and speaking engagements.

## CONTACT

www.briellevalleconsulting.com

# NOTES

**Introduction**

11 World Health Organization. (2020, March 11). *WHO Director-General's opening remarks at the mediabriefing on COVID-19.* https://www.who.int/director-general/speeches/detail/who-director-general-s-opening-remarks-at-the-media-briefing-on-covid-19---11-march-2020

**I: America's <Promising> Dream**

15 Diamond, A. (2018, October 01). *The original meanings of the "American Dream" and "America First" were starkly different from how we use them today.* Smithsonian Magazine. https://www.smithsonianmag.com/history/behold-america-american-dream-slogan-book-sarah-churchwell-180970311/

16 Abrams, S. (2019, February 05). The American dream is alive and well. *New York Times.* https://www.nytimes.com/2019/02/05/opinion/american-dream.html

17 Ganger, B. (2008). Women and language. *Journal of communication* 32(1), 104-115.

18 Fine, M. (2009). Women leaders' discursive constructions of leadership. *Journal of women's studies in communication*, 32(2), 180-202. https://doi.org/10.1080/07491409.2009.10162386

19 Identity. (2020). In *Merriam-Webster.com*. Retrieved January 15, 2021, from https://www.merriam-webster.com/dictionary/identity

**II: Working From Home: An Anomaly Changed Necessity**

24 Gregg, M. (2008). The normalization of flexible female labour in the information economy. *Feminist Media Studies*, 8(3), 285-299. https://doi.org/10.1080/14680770802217311

24 Edwards, P. & Wajcman, J. (2005). *The politics of a working life.* NY: Oxford University Press Inc.

25 Gershon, L. (2020, October 19). *Covid-19's impact on working women is an*

unprecedented disaster. Smithsonian Magazine. https://www.smithsonianmag.com/smart-news/covid-19s-impact-working-women-unprecedented-disaster-180976084/

29 Coury, S., Huang, J., Kumar, A., Prince, S., Krivkovich, A., & Yee, L. (2020, September 30). *Women in the workplace.* McKinsey & Company. https://www.mckinsey.com/featured-insights/diversity-and-inclusion/women-in-the-workplace

29 Kerin, R., Lundstrom, W., & Sciglimpaglia, D. (1979). Women in advertisements: Retrospect and prospect. *Journal of Advertising*, 8(3), 37-42. https://doi.org/10.1080/00913367.1979.10673287

30 McCartney, S. (2020, November 04). How coronavirus ravaged travel in 2020. *Wall Street Journal.* https://www.wsj.com/articles/how-coronavirus-ravaged-travel-in-2020-11604500952

## III: Default to Responsibility

32 Feldman, R., & Bakermans-Kranenburg, M. (2017, February 20). *Oxytocin: A parenting hormone.* Science Direct. https://www.sciencedirect.com/science/article/pii/S2352250X17300325

33 Kersting, L. (2004, August). *Brain research advances help elucidate teen behavior.* American Psychological Association. https://www.apa.org/monitor/julaug04/brain

33 Yogman, M., & Garfield, C. (2016, July 01). *Fathers' roles in the care and development of their children: The role of pediatricians.* Pediatrics. https://pediatrics.aappublications.org/content/138/1/e20161128

34 Brenan, M. (2021, January 14). *Women still handle main household tasks in U.S.* Gallup. https://news.gallup.com/poll/283979/women-handle-main-household-tasks.aspx

35 Collins, C. (2019). *Making motherhood work: How women manage careers and caregiving.* Princeton, NJ: Princeton University Press.

37 Coury, S., Huang, J., Kumar, A., Prince, S., Krivkovich, A., & Yee, L. (2020, September 30). *Women in the workplace.* McKinsey & Company. https://www.mckinsey.com/featured-insights/diversity-and-inclusion/women-in-the-workplace

38 Cutruzzula, K., & Brooks, R. (2020, October 01). *6 things we can learn from how*

women leaders have handled the pandemic. TED Ideas. https://ideas.ted.com/6-things-we-can-learn-from-how-women-leaders-have-handled-the-pandemic/

39 Stillman, J. (2021, January 07). *New research: Women leaders performed better during the covid crisis.* Inc. https://apple.news/A7qDwnVQcSQSLBHsknzFc7A

39 Kurtz, A. (2021, January 09). *The US economy lost 140,000 jobs in December. All of them were held by women.* CNN. https://www.cnn.com/2021/01/08/economy/women-job-losses-pandemic/index.html

39 Barrett, B. (2020, December 14). Performance management must evolve to survive covid-19. Gallup. https://www.gallup.com/workplace/318029/performance-management-evolve-survive-covid.aspx

42 The Riveter. (2020, November 23). *Riveter x Vice: The covid-19 double shift.* https://theriveter.co/voice/riveter-x-vice-the-covid-19-double-shift/

**IV: Culture and Upbringing**

46 Galimberti, G. (n.d.). *Toy Stories.* https://www.gabrielegalimberti.com/toy-stories/

47 Kay, K., & Shipman, C. (2018). *The confidence code: The science and art of self-assurance---What women should know.* New York, NY: HarperCollins Publishers.

47 Pazzanese, C. (2020, February 11). Women less inclined to self-promote than men, even for a job. Harvard Gazette. https://news.harvard.edu/gazette/story/2020/02/men-better-than-women-at-self-promotion-on-job-leading-to-inequities/

48 Coury, S., Huang, J., Kumar, A., Prince, S., Krivkovich, A., & Yee, L. (2020, September 30). *Women in the workplace.* McKinsey & Company. https://www.mckinsey.com/featured-insights/diversity-and-inclusion/women-in-the-workplace

51 Valenti, J. (2018, July 27). *Not wanting kids is entirely normal.* The Atlantic. https://www.theatlantic.com/health/archive/2012/09/not-wanting-kids-is-entirely-normal/262367/

52 Gallagher, J. (2020, July 14). *Fertility rate: 'Jaw-dropping' global crash in children being born.* BBC. https://www.bbc.com/news/health-53409521

52 Hewlett, S. (2002). Executive women and the myth of having it all. *Harvard business review,* 80(4), 66-73.

## V: An Independent Life

58 Kavin, K. (2020, August 15). Dog adoptions and sales soar during the pandemic. *Washington Post.* https://www.washingtonpost.com/nation/2020/08/12/adoptions-dogs-coronavirus/

## VI: Persistent Inequities

61 Brownwell, T. (2020, October 16). *Divorce rates and covid-19.* The National Law Review. https://www.natlawreview.com/article/divorce-rates-and-covid-19

64 National Partnership for Women & Families. (2020, September). *America's women and the wage gap.* https://www.nationalpartnership.org/our-work/resources/economic-justice/fair-pay/americas-women-and-the-wage-gap.pdf

65 National Partnership for Women & Families. (2020, September). *America's women and the wage gap.* https://www.nationalpartnership.org/our-work/resources/economic-justice/fair-pay/americas-women-and-the-wage-gap.pdf

68 Jean-Philippe, M. (2021, January 21). Read 22-year-old Amanda Gorman's breathtaking inauguration poem. Oprah Magazine. https://www.oprahmag.com/entertainment/a35268319/amanda-gorman-inauguration-poem-transcript/

68 Semuels, A. (2020, June 19). *How segregation contributes to the racial wealth gap.* TIME. https://time.com/5855900/segregation-wealth-gap/

70 McRae, K., Ochsner, K., Mauss, I., Gabrieli, J., & Gross, J. (2008). Gender differences in emotion regulation: An fMRI study of cognitive reappraisal. *Group Process & Intergroup Relations, 11*(2), 143-162. https://doi.org/10.1177/1368430207088035

## VII: A Reliant Life

73 Sample, I. (2020, December 27). *Covid poses 'greatest threat to mental health since second world war.* The Guardian. https://www.theguardian.com/society/2020/dec/27/covid-poses-greatest-threat-to-mental-health-since-second-world-war

## VIII: Where We Go From Here

80 National Partnership for Women & Families. (2020, September). *America's women*

*and the wage gap.* https://www.nationalpartnership.org/our-work/resources/economic-justice/fair-pay/americas-women-and-the-wage-gap.pdf

81 Lake, R. (2020, March 31). *How long does maternity leave last?* The Balance Careers. https://www.thebalancecareers.com/how-long-is-the-average-maternity-leave-4590252

81 Almes, B. (2019, December 09). New DDI research: 57 percent of employees quit because of their boss. PR Newswire. https://www.prnewswire.com/news-releases/new-ddi-research-57-percent-of-employees-quit-because-of-their-boss-300971506.html#:~:text=Key%20findings%20in%20the%20research,job%20because%20of%20their%20 manager

81 The Riveter. (2020, November 23). *Riveter x Vice: The covid-19 double shift.* https://theriveter.co/voice/riveter-x-vice-the-covid-19-double-shift/

83 The Riveter. (2020, November 23). *Riveter x Vice: The covid-19 double shift.* https://theriveter.co/voice/riveter-x-vice-the-covid-19-double-shift/